DOUBLEDAY THEATER SERIES

SUITE IN THREE KEYS

Montage of the London production of *Suite in Three Keys*

SUITE IN THREE KEYS

A Song at Twilight

Shadows of the Evening

Come into the Garden Maud

by
NOËL COWARD

DOUBLEDAY & COMPANY, INC.   GARDEN CITY, NEW YORK   1967

Library of Congress Catalog Card Number 67–11022
Copyright © 1966 by Noël Coward
All Rights Reserved
Printed in the United States of America
First Edition in the United States of America

A Song at Twilight was first presented by H. M. Tennent Ltd. at the Queen's Theatre, London, on April 25, 1966. Shadows of the Evening and Come into the Garden Maud were first performed at the same theatre on April 14, 1966. The cast was as follows:

NOËL COWARD

LILLI PALMER

IRENE WORTH

SEAN BARRETT

Directed by Vivian Matalon
Setting by Brian Currah
Costumes by Molyneux-Paris
Lighting by Joe Davis

A SONG AT TWILIGHT

A Comedy in Two Acts

For Doctor Edward Bigg
with love and gratitude

A SONG AT TWILIGHT

CAST OF CHARACTERS

Hilde Latymer	IRENE WORTH
Felix, a waiter	SEAN BARRETT
Hugo Latymer	NOËL COWARD
Carlotta Gray	LILLI PALMER

The time is the present. The action of the play passes in a private suite of the Hotel Beau Rivage, Lausanne-Ouchy, Switzerland.

ACT I

The action of the play passes in a private suite in a luxurious hotel in Switzerland.

The scene is the sitting room. The suite is occupied for two or three months each year by SIR HUGO LATYMER, *an elderly writer of considerable eminence.*

The conventional hotel furnishing has been augmented by some of SIR HUGO's *personal possessions which include an impressive writing desk, a special armchair by the side of which is a small table. On this are books, bottles of medicine and pills, a small gold clock and a slim vase containing a number of ball-point pens. On the walls hang some of* SIR HUGO's *favourite Impressionist paintings.*

On stage Left there is a door leading into the bedroom. There are double doors at the back which open onto a small lobby and then the corridor. HILDE's *room also opens off the lobby.*

HILDE LATYMER *is a faded woman in her early fifties. She has been married to* SIR HUGO *for nearly twenty years and was originally his secretary. Apart from being his official German translator, she is capable, dedicated, and orders his life with considerable efficiency.*

When the curtain rises she is seated at the writing desk. Standing near her is FELIX, *the floor-waiter. He is a startlingly handsome young man of about twenty-eight and there is already in his manner that subtle blend of obsequiousness, authority, and charm which, if he does not allow his good looks to lead him astray, will ultimately carry him to the top of his profession. At the moment he is holding a notebook and listening to* HILDE *with polite attention.*

9

HILDE

That will be all for the moment, Felix. Sir Hugo's guest is due at eight o'clock but it is possible that she might be a little late so I think you should be prepared to serve the dinner at about eight-thirty but not before.

FELIX

A touch of garlic in the salad dressing as usual?

HILDE

Yes. But only the smallest touch. We don't want a repetition of last Friday, do we?

FELIX

Friday night is much to be regretted, milady. But if you will remember I was off duty. Giovanni is a most willing boy but he is not yet accustomed to Sir Hugo's tastes.

HILDE

You will warn him to be more careful next time.

FELIX

Very good, milady. (*He bows and goes out*)

HILDE

(*lifting the telephone. She speaks with a rather heavy German accent*)
'Allo, mademoiselle. J'ai demandè un prèavis a Londres il y a presq'une demi'heure. Est ce que vous en avez des nouvelles? Oui —Oui, merci, j'attendrai.
(*She hangs up the receiver and devotes her attention to some letters on the desk. After a moment or two the telephone rings*)
Hallo—is that you, Carl? This is Hilde Latymer speaking. I have been trying to get you all the afternoon. First of all regarding the

10

lecture tour in the States . . . Yes I know . . . But Sir Hugo really
isn't up to it . . . Oh yes, he is much better but the doctor insists
that my husband must not undertake anything that is not absolutely necessary. Yes. He will accept the doctorate at the uni-
versity and make a speech as arranged, but nothing more than
that. After it's over we will either come straight back here or go
to Arizona for a rest . . . No I am truly sorry but it can't be helped
. . . No, he's resting at the moment otherwise he would speak to
you himself . . . Now then, regarding the film proposition for
The Winding River. You will have to put in the contract that he
has complete veto on the script and the adaptor. Well he certainly won't sign it unless that is confirmed in writing . . . On
the contrary I think it matters a great deal. It involves his name
and reputation . . .

(*At this moment* SIR HUGO LATYMER *comes out of the bedroom. He is a distinguished-looking elderly man. His figure is
slim and erect. Sometimes, when he is in a good mood he
looks younger than he actually is by several years. At other
times, when upset over some triviality or worried about his
health, he becomes suddenly enfeebled and deliberately ancient. This of course is a pose but it works like a charm on
doctors and nurses or whoever happens to be looking after
him at the moment. It even works on* HILDE *occasionally not-
withstanding the fact that she has had twenty years to grow
accustomed to it.*

SIR HUGO *is wearing a dressing gown, his white hair is
slightly tousled and he looks irascible.*)

HUGO

What involves my name and reputation?

HILDE

(*putting her hand over the telephone*)
It's Carl. We're talking about *The Winding River* contract.

11

HUGO

Then you are both wasting your time. I have no intention of sign-
ing it whatever concessions they make.

HILDE

But Hugo dear, you did say that providing they gave you complete
veto of script and adaptor that—

HUGO

(*snappily*)

Well, I have changed my mind. I have had no less than three
novels and five of my best short stories massacred by that cretinous
medium. I refuse to have any more of it.

HILDE

(*at telephone*)

I can't talk any more at the moment, Carl. Ring me in the morning at eleven o'clock . . . Very well, ten o'clock but be sure to
have it put through to my room. Yes, 355. Good-bye. (*She hangs
up*)

HUGO

(*sitting in his chair*)

Carl's getting out of hand. He needs a serious talking to. All he
thinks about is his damned percentage.

HILDE

You can't altogether blame him for that. He *is* your agent.

HUGO

What time is it?

HILDE

(*glancing at her watch*)

Nearly half-past seven. Isn't that clock going?

HUGO

I haven't the faintest idea. It's so exquisitely made that I can't see it without my glasses.

HILDE

You said you were delighted with it when I gave it to you.

HUGO

Well, I'm not now.

HILDE

I'm sorry. I'll try and change it.

HUGO

And please don't look martyred. It draws your mouth down at the corners. Like a weary old camel.

HILDE

Thank you.

HUGO

With two unsymmetrical humps.

HILDE

That's a dromedary. Have you had your bath?

HUGO

No, I have not had my bath.

HILDE

Well, don't you think you should? She's due at eight.

HUGO

If I'm not ready she can wait for me, can't she? An extra ten minutes tacked onto all those years can't matter all that much.

(*The telephone rings.*)

Damn that bloody instrument! Why can't you have it switched into your room and go and sit by it?

HILDE

You're in a very disagreeable mood.

HUGO

I'm nervous.

HILDE

It's your own fault if you are. You needn't have agreed to see her. (*The telephone rings again.*)

HUGO

For God's sake answer it.

HILDE

(*lifting the receiver*)

'Allo 'allo. Oui, à l'appareil . . . Mariette, c'est vous! Non je ne suis pas certain, si vous voudrez attendre pour un petit moment je vais voir. (*She puts her hand over the receiver*) It's Mariette.

HUGO

Curiously enough I gathered that. Why didn't you say I was out?

HILDE

I can still say you're being massaged.

HUGO

You said that last time. She'll think I spend my whole life being massaged. Here—give it to me . . .

HILDE

(*into telephone*)

Un instant, Mariette. (*She brings the telephone over to his chair*)

14

HUGO

(*his French of course is excellent*)
*Ma chere Mariette—enfin! Je suis absolument ravi d'entendre ta
voix. Comment va tu?* . . . Alas no, my dear I cannot possibly. I
already have a rendézvous this evening. No, no, not that kind at
all . . . No, this is a rendézvous with the past, the very very far
distant past . . . No, no nobody you've ever heard of. It was all
over and done with before you were born . . . Not another word,
I have said far too much as it is . . . Very well, luncheon on Tuesday. (*He raises his eyebrows at* HILDE *who glances quickly at his
engagement pad and nods*) Until Tuesday . . . A *bientot chérie.*
(*he hangs up*)
  (HILDE *relieves him of the telephone and takes it back to the
  desk.*)
There was no getting out of that. I've put her off three times in
the last month. You're looking sour, Hilde. What's the matter
now?

HILDE

I think you were indiscreet.

HUGO

Stop nagging at me.

HILDE

It is not nagging to say that I think you are indiscreet.

HUGO

(*with almost a conscious smirk*)
I have been feeling indiscreet all day.

HILDE

Have you indeed?

15

HUGO

Yes. And wrapped in an agreeable anticipatory glow until your screeching down the telephone woke me from my nap.

HILDE

Mariette is the most incorrigible gossip. Do you want the whole of Switzerland to know about your private affairs?

HUGO

Switzerland must have a pretty shrewd idea of them by now anyway.

HILDE

I was not speaking financially.

HUGO

(*with a complacent smile*)

No, Hilde, I didn't think you were.

HILDE

Do go and have your bath and dress.

HUGO

I only said I had a rendézvous with the past, which is perfectly true, I have.

HILDE

You made it sound furtive, almost romantic.

HUGO

Perhaps it will be.

HILDE

You would wish it to be romantic?

16

HUGO

No, Hilde, I have long ago given up wishing that anything could be romantic.

HILDE

I find it difficult to believe that you ever did.

HUGO

(*irritably*)

Ever did what?

HILDE

Sigh for the moon and the stars, open your heart to illusion.

HUGO

I admit that I have always preferred realism to fantasy.

HILDE

Even when you were young and in love—with Carlotta?

HUGO

Even then.

HILDE

I still think all this is a great mistake.

HUGO

Yes, I know you do. You've made that abundantly clear during the last three days. You've never been exactly adept at hiding your feelings.

HILDE

On the contrary, Hugo, that is one of the things I do best. Living with you for twenty years has been excellent training.

17

HUGO

Why are you so frightened of Carlotta?

HILDE

(*calmly*)

I am not in the least frightened of Carlotta.

HUGO

Oh yes you are. The very idea of her fills your soul with dread. Come on now, admit it.

HILDE

It is time for your blue pill. (*She goes abruptly into the bedroom leaving the door open*)

HUGO

(*enjoying himself*)

You'd better take a tranquilliser to calm your desperate fears.

HILDE

(*returning with a pill and a glass of water*)

Whatever fears I may have about Carlotta are entirely on your account. She is bound to upset you in some way or other. She wouldn't suddenly reappear in your life like this unless she wanted something. Here you are. (*She hands him the pill*)

HUGO

(*taking it*)

Perhaps she wants a reunion.

HILDE

Money more likely. She has not been very successful during the last fifteen years.

HUGO

Have you been following her career?

18

HILDE
(taking the glass)
There hasn't been much career to follow lately. (*She goes off into the bedroom again*)

HUGO
(complacently)
Poor Carlotta!

HILDE
(returning)
She will upset you. I feel it in my bones. It is like the weather. I can always tell when it is going to rain.

HUGO
That particular form of prescience is rheumatic rather than clairvoyant. In any case it is within the bounds of possibility that I might upset her.

HILDE
She doesn't suffer from your particular form of nervous indigestion.

HUGO
She might be riddled with ulcers for all you know.

HILDE
She didn't sound as if she were on the telephone.

HUGO
Why should she? Gastric ulcers have little or no relation to the vocal chords.

HILDE
(turning away)
I will say no more.

19

HUGO

Turn round, Hilde. I don't like talking to your back. It's such a Teutonic, uncompromising back.

HILDE
(*turning*)

Is that better?

HUGO

Give me your hand.
(HILDE *comes over to him reluctantly. He takes her hand and looks up at her with a quizzical smile. The charm is on.*)

HILDE

A lump of sugar for a good little dog?

HUGO
(*letting her hand go*)

I see you're determined to be tiresome.

HILDE

It's unfair of you to say that. It's you I'm thinking of. You've been so much better lately. Dr. Benoist says your blood pressure is back to normal, you're sleeping well and you haven't had any pains for three weeks. I just don't want you to have a relapse. You know that any sort of excitement is bad for you.

HUGO

Do you seriously believe that seeing Carlotta again will excite me to the extent of sending up my blood pressure?

HILDE

You've been giving every indication of it.

HUGO

Oh, Hilde—Hilde. What an egregious ass you are.

HILDE

You have now called me a camel, a dromedary and an ass within
the last ten minutes. Your normal dialogue is less zoological. You
have worked yourself up into a state about seeing Carlotta again
and it's no use pretending you haven't. I know the symptoms. I
haven't been with you for twenty years for nothing.

HUGO

Am I so transparent?

HILDE

To me—yes.

HUGO
(*petulantly*)

It's you who are sending my blood pressure up, not Carlotta . . .
Give me a cigarette.

HILDE
(*reluctantly handing him a cigarette box*)

It will be your seventh today.

HUGO

No, it won't, it will be my sixth. I only had one after lunch.

HILDE
(*lighting a cigarette for him*)

Be careful. That's all I ask of you. Just be careful. She made you
unhappy before. I don't want you to give her the chance of making you unhappy again.

HUGO
(*patiently*)

Now listen to me, Hilde. My affair with Carlotta lasted exactly
two years and we parted in a blaze of mutual acrimony. That was

21

many years ago and I haven't clapped eyes on her since except once on the cinema screen when she appeared briefly as a Mother Superior in an excruciatingly bad film about a nun with a vast bust. Nor have we corresponded. This sudden request on her part to see me again has not unnaturally filled me with curiosity. It is quite possible that your surmise is right and that she wants to borrow money. If that is so I will lend her some for old time's sake. On the other hand she may merely want to see me for sentimental reasons. Time and the difficult years may have mellowed her, or she may even wish to gloat over my age and infirmity.

HILDE
(*sharply*)

You are *not* infirm.

HUGO

After all you must remember that she was very much in love with me.

HILDE

And you with her?

HUGO

Of course.

HILDE

Was she beautiful?

HUGO

Not in the classical sense. But she was extremely attractive and her vitality was inexhaustible.

HILDE

I suspect that it still is.

22

HUGO

Even so, the chances of a passionate, physical reunion are remote.

HILDE

So I should hope. The very idea would be ridiculous.

HUGO

Not quite so ridiculous as all that. Anyhow you cannot deny that the possibility crossed your mind.

HILDE
(*hotly*)

I most certainly do deny it.

HUGO

Isn't that overvehemence a trifle suspect?

HILDE

Suspect! What do you mean?

HUGO

Quite frankly, I suspect you of being jealous.

HILDE
(*quietly*)

No, Hugo, I am not jealous. I realised many years ago that I had no right to be jealous.

HUGO

Since when has jealousy been so law-abiding? Is it an emotion that obediently sticks to the rules?

HILDE

I have no wish to argue with you.

23

HUGO

You are jealous of all my friends, of anyone who is close to me, and you always have been.

HILDE

(*with a show of spirit*)

You have not so many friends for me to be jealous of.

HUGO

You hate Mariette. You are barely civil to Cedric Marcombe and David when they come here.

HILDE

They are barely civil to me.

HUGO

Cedric Marcombe is a man of brilliant intelligence and exquisite taste. He is also the greatest connoisseur of modern art alive today.

HILDE

And what is David?

HUGO

(*defensively*)

David is one of the most promising young painters that England has produced in the last twenty years, he also happens to be the son of Lord Tenterden.

HILDE

In that case he should have better manners. And his paintings I do not care for at all. They are ugly and cruel.

HUGO

(*viciously*)

As a full-blooded German you are scarcely in a position to object to cruelty in art or anything else.

HILDE

It is wrong of you to speak to me like that, Hugo, and most unkind. When you are in a better mood you will see that this is so and be sorry. In any case this sort of argument is waste of time and energy. You cannot, after all these long years, seriously imagine that I am jealous of your friends or your heart. If I am jealous at all it is for your well-being. You really must try not to get cross so easily. You know what it does to your acids. Remember what Dr. Benoist said.

HUGO

Now you're talking like a district nurse.

HILDE

No district nurse would have had the endurance to put up with your sudden tempers for as long as I have.

HUGO

Do you wish to leave me? Are you giving me a month's notice?

HILDE

If I wished to leave you I should have done so long ago. Now it is too late.

HUGO

For God's sake stop looking hurt, Hilde. It infuriates me.

HILDE

If you do not wish me to look hurt you should not try so hard to hurt me. I do my best to help you with the business of your life, even to love you as far as you will allow me to. But you make it most difficult for me, sometimes almost too difficult to be borne. (*She turns away*)

HUGO

Oh Lord! Now I suppose you are going to cry.

HILDE

(*turning*)

No, Hugo. I am not going to cry. That too is waste of time and
energy. I am going to put on my hat.

HUGO

(*realising that he has gone too far*)

Hilde . . .

HILDE

If you are determined to receive your long lost love in a dressing
gown with your hair all rumpled, that is entirely your affair.

HUGO

Hilde, I'm sorry. I'm sorry that I upset you.

HILDE

It is nothing new.

HUGO

I am beginning to feel those palpitations again.

HILDE

I am not surprised.

HUGO

I wonder what she looks like? She's been in America most of her
life. She'll probably have bright blue hair. Or else she'll be defeated and grey and bedraggled and make me feel old.

HILDE

Do not be foolish. You know perfectly well that you only feel old
when you wish to.

(HUGO *rises and goes over to the window.*)

HUGO

I don't feel now that I can face her alone. You'd better stay after all.

HILDE

Certainly not. I've already arranged to dine with Liesel at the Grappe d'Or and go to a cinema afterwards.

HUGO

Liesel is a weather-beaten old German lesbian.

HILDE

She is also highly intelligent.

HUGO

Is she in love with you?

HILDE

Not in the least. She lives with a Chinese student who paints butterflies on glass.

HUGO

Whatever for?

HILDE

Actually she's very talented.

HUGO

Put Liesel off . . . don't go . . . Stay with me, I need your support.

HILDE

I can't. She's already booked the tickets and reserved a table.

HUGO

Cut the film then and come straight back here after dinner.

HILDE

(*firmly*)

No, Hugo. You've brought this situation on yourself and you will have to deal with it yourself.

HUGO

You have ordered the dinner?

HILDE

Yes. Felix will bring it when you ring.

HUGO

I think I should like a drink, to fortify me.

HILDE

I'll ring for some ice. (*She does so*) It had better be vodka. You're having it with the caviar anyhow.

HUGO

I never told you to order caviar.

HILDE

No. It was my own idea. I ordered pink champagne too.

HUGO

Pink champagne! Good God. Why?

HILDE

You're always accusing me of not having a sense of humour. I thought I'd like to prove you wrong.

HUGO

Is the rest of the menu equally plutocratic?

28

HILDE

No, comparatively simple. Steak Bearnaise, green salad, and a chocolate soufflé.

HUGO

I shan't sleep a wink.

HILDE

I shouldn't count too much on that anyhow. The Maalox tablets are in the table drawer if you should need them.
(FELIX *enters with a bucket of ice.*)
Give Sir Hugo a vodka on the rocks, will you, Felix?

FELIX

Very good, milady.

HILDE
(*at the door*)
I won't be more than a few minutes. (*She goes*)

HUGO
(*with charm*)
I missed you sadly last evening, Felix. Where did you disappear to?

FELIX
(*mixing the drink*)
It was my half-day off, sir.

HUGO

Your substitute lacked charm, he also breathed like an old locomotive.

FELIX

That was Giovanni, sir. He comes from Calabria.

29

HUGO

The railway journey must have made a profound impression on him.

FELIX

Your vodka, sir. (*He hands it to him*)

HUGO

Thank you. Did you enjoy your half-day off?

FELIX

Oh yes, sir. We went to swim in the piscine at Vevey, it is not so crowded as the one here, and then we came back and went to a movie.

HUGO

We?

FELIX

My friend and I. He is the assistant barman at the Hotel de la Paix. He is a champion swimmer and has won many trophies.

HUGO

You look as though you should be a good swimmer yourself, with those shoulders.

FELIX

Not as good as he is, but I myself love to water-ski, it is a great sport.

HUGO

It must be. Water-skiing was not invented when I was your age. (*He hears* HILDE *returning*) Thank you, Felix. You will bring the dinner when I ring?

FELIX

Very good, sir.

HUGO

It should be in about half an hour's time, depending on when my guest arrives.

FELIX

Bien, monsieur. (*He bows and goes*)

HILDE

Are you feeling more relaxed?

HUGO

More resigned at any rate. That's quite a masculine-looking little hat, almost a bowler. Are you wearing it as a subtle gesture to your hostess?

HILDE

You know I dislike that sort of joke, Hugo. Liesel has been a good friend of mine for many years. I am very fond of her. The other side of her life is of no interest to me.

HUGO

Give me another cigarette.

HILDE

Certainly not! You've already had too many today.

HUGO

I tell you I'm nervous.

HILDE

Such nonsense. You will probably have a most delightful evening, looking back into the past, remembering little jokes . . .

HUGO

(*interrupting her*)

Why have you so suddenly changed your attitude? A short while ago you were moaning and groaning and saying that you didn't want me to see Carlotta again because she would upset me and probably give me a relapse. Now you seem determined to turn the whole occasion into a sort of gruesome "gala" with your damned caviar and vodka and pink champagne.

HILDE

I've changed my mind. I think she might do you good.
(*The telephone rings.*)

HUGO

There now!

HILDE

(*answering it*)

Oui, Gaston. Demandez a Madame de monter toute de suite.
(*She hangs up*)

HUGO

The tiresome woman is early.

HILDE

No. It is you who are late. Go quickly. It would be inelegant to receive an ex-mistress in your dressing gown, however old she is. I will talk to her until you are ready—go along.

HUGO

Promise me you'll cut the cinema and come straight back here after dinner.

HILDE

That all depends. I'll think about it. Go along—hurry.
(HUGO *goes into the bedroom. There is a knock at the door.*

HILDE *goes to open it.* CARLOTTA GRAY *comes into the room. She is an attractive woman who at first glance would appear to be in her late forties or early fifties. She is heavily made up and her hair is expertly tinted. She is wearing expensive costume jewellery, perhaps a little too much of it. Her dinner dress is simple and well cut and she carries a light coat over her arm.*)

HILDE
(*holding out her hand*)
I am Hilde Latymer. How do you do.

CARLOTTA
(*taking it*)
Of course. I recognize your voice. You were so kind on the telephone.

HILDE
My husband is dressing, he won't be more than a few minutes. May I take your coat?

CARLOTTA
(*handing it to her*)
Thank you.

HILDE
Please be so kind as to sit down and take a cigarette if you should care to smoke. They are in that tortoise-shell box.
(HILDE *disappears into the bedroom with the coat.* CARLOTTA *goes to the box, takes a cigarette and lights it, and looks round the room.* HILDE *returns, closing the bedroom door carefully behind her.*)

CARLOTTA
What a delightful "Renoir" . . . and a "Boudin" too! His skies are always so lovely, aren't they?

33

HILDE

You are interested in painting?

CARLOTTA

Oh yes, immensely interested, but I fear not very knowledgeable.

HILDE

Would you care for a drink?

CARLOTTA

Perhaps not quite yet. I would rather wait a little. How is he, Hugo? (*She corrects herself*) Sir Hugo?

HILDE

He is almost completely well again. He has of course to take care not to overdo things and not to become agitated or unduly excited. He has always been nervously overstrung, as you may probably remember.

CARLOTTA

I don't remember him being overstrung exactly. On the contrary his studied calmness used occasionally to irritate me. It was as though he had made a private vow to remain Captain of his Soul no matter what emotional hurricanes he might encounter. But it was all so long long ago. He has had ample time to change, as indeed we all have.

HILDE

(*with a faint smile*)

I agree that Hugo has not the sort of temperament to be easily battered by "emotional hurricanes" as you put it, but that is not quite what I meant.

CARLOTTA

He has certainly had a wonderful career. It wouldn't be surprising if he sometimes found the burden of his eminence a trifle nerve-wracking.

CARLOTTA

HILDE

(*not quite pleased with this either*)

Nerve-wracking?

CARLOTTA

The continual demands made upon his time, the constant strain of having to live up to the self-created image he has implanted in the public mind. How fortunate he is to have you to protect him.

HILDE

(*stiffly*)

He isn't, I think, in quite such urgent need of protection as you imagine.

CARLOTTA

You've been married for twenty years, haven't you?

HILDE

Yes. He engaged me as his secretary in January 1945, and a few months later we were married.

CARLOTTA

(*smiling*)

I remember the headlines. It caused quite a sensation.

HILDE

(*turning away*)

Yes, I know it did. There was much foolishness written in the papers.

CARLOTTA

You are not in the least like I thought you'd be.

35

HILDE

(*politely*)

Indeed? What did you expect?

CARLOTTA

Someone more grim, less vulnerable. A dragon guarding the throne.

HILDE

You put things so picturesquely, Miss Gray. Perhaps you should have been a writer yourself.

CARLOTTA

The idea has crossed my mind. Hugo used to accuse me of being garrulous and overarticulate long ago. How does he feel about seeing me again, after so long?

HILDE

I cannot say. He is curious, naturally.

CARLOTTA

And you? What are your reactions to this—this rather peculiar situation?

HILDE

I have no feelings about it one way or the other.

CARLOTTA

I will accept the snub but I am not entirely convinced by it.

HILDE

It was not intended to be a snub. You will please forgive me?

CARLOTTA

There is nothing whatever to forgive. I find it perfectly understandable that you should be suspicious of me. It is the duty of

36

even the kindliest protective dragons to be wary of strangers. It is sad that we did not meet in earlier, different circumstances. We might have been friends.

HILDE
(*melting a trifle*)
Thank you, Miss Gray.
(HUGO *comes out of the bedroom. He is wearing an emerald green velvet smoking jacket over dark trousers. He has a cream silk shirt, a black tie and his slippers are monogrammed in gold.* CARLOTTA *rises and looks at him for a moment. Then she goes to him.*)

CARLOTTA
Hugo! What a strange moment this is, isn't it? I had planned so many things to say and now they've gone clean out of my head. Do we embrace?

HUGO
(*with a slightly self-conscious smile*)
Why not? (*He kisses her formally on both cheeks*)

CARLOTTA
(*drawing away*)
How well you look! Slim as ever and so distinguished. White hair definitely becomes you.

HUGO
(*with splendid chivalry*)
The years seem to have forgotten you, Carlotta.

CARLOTTA
Oh no, my dear. It isn't that they have forgotten me, it's that I have remembered them and taken the right precautions.

37

HUGO

You and Hilde have already made friends I see.

CARLOTTA

(*glancing swiftly at* HILDE)

Yes. As a matter of fact we have. (*to* HILDE) It's been puzzling me where I could have seen you before but now I remember. There's a photograph of you in Hugo's autobiography. You are leaning against a pillar and shading your eyes with your hand as though you were worried about the weather.

HUGO

The pillar was one of the columns of the Parthenon.

HILDE

The light was very strong.

CARLOTTA

Alas. There is no photograph of me in the book. At least, only a verbal one. (*She looks at* HUGO) The light was a little too strong in that too.

HUGO

Can I offer you a drink?

CARLOTTA

Oh yes, by all means. I should love one.

HILDE

(*going to the drink table*)

Whisky, brandy, gin, vodka?

CARLOTTA

Vodka please, on the rocks. (*to* HUGO) I expected you to look much older. But that's beside the point nowadays, isn't it? I mean—

people hardly ever look their real age any more. Time is learning to accept a few defeats. It's rather fun frustrating the old monster.

HILDE
(*bringing her drink*)
Your vodka, Miss Gray.

CARLOTTA
Thank you so much.

HILDE
(*to* CARLOTTA)
I am afraid I must leave you now. I have a dinner engagement.

CARLOTTA
Oh, how disappointing. I had hoped to get to know you better.

HILDE
We shall probably meet again.

CARLOTTA
Of course. We're almost bound to. I have moved into this hotel.

HILDE
(*caught unawares*)
Oh!

CARLOTTA
(*putting out her hand*)
Don't be alarmed. I shall only be here for a few days. I am having a series of injections at the clinique and it's more convenient to be here than in Vevey.

HILDE
(*shaking her hand*)
Au revoir then, Miss Gray.

39

CARLOTTA
(*smiling*)

A *bientot*, Lady Latymer.
(HILDE *shoots an equivocal look at* HUGO *and goes swiftly out of the room.* CARLOTTA *strolls over to the window.*)

CARLOTTA

How lovely it is with the lights glittering in the distance. I went over to Evian the other evening on the little steamer and won nearly a thousand francs.

HUGO
(*slightly shocked*)

Can you afford to play so high?

CARLOTTA

Oh yes. I have a certain amount put by. I also still get alimony from my last husband.

HUGO

Have you had many others?

CARLOTTA

Two before this one. They both died. One in an air crash and the other in the war.

HUGO

Did you love them?

CARLOTTA

Oh yes. I shouldn't have married them if I hadn't.

HUGO

Have you any children?

40

CARLOTTA

Yes. I had a son by my second husband. He's twenty-four now and very attractive. You'd love him. He's an entomologist.

HUGO

I don't believe I've ever met an entomologist. That's insects, isn't it?

CARLOTTA

Yes. There's a great deal more in insects than meets the eye.

HUGO

I'm sure there is. Personally I've never felt particularly drawn to them.

CARLOTTA

I expect you thought that the bombardier beetle shoots compressed air from its intestines, whereas in actual fact it is highly explosive rocket fuel which it produces in two of its glands.

HUGO

I must admit that has been baffling me for some time.

CARLOTTA

And grasshoppers! You must like grasshoppers!

HUGO

I'm sorry to disappoint you, but I don't.

CARLOTTA

They converse by rubbing their back legs together.

HUGO

I'm beginning to wish we did.

CARLOTTA

Am I to drink alone?

HUGO

Too much alcohol is bad for me.

CARLOTTA

Too much alcohol is bad for everyone. Just pour yourself a teeny weeny one to keep me company.

HUGO

Really, Carlotta, you're too absurd.

CARLOTTA

She's nice, your wife. I like her.

HUGO

I'm so glad.

CARLOTTA

In spite of the fact that she doesn't care for me much. I don't think you quite did her justice in your book. But then, you weren't very nice about anybody in your book, were you?

HUGO

You were under no obligation to read it.

CARLOTTA

There was no warning on the cover. You take a fairly jaundiced view of your fellow creatures, don't you, on the whole?

HUGO

Perhaps. I prefer to see people as they are rather than as more sentimental minds would wish them to be. However, I am a commentator, not a moralist. I state no preferences.

CARLOTTA

Admirable!

HUGO

I would hate you to imagine that I am unaware of the mocking expression in your eye.

CARLOTTA
(*with a smile*)

Don't worry. I would never suspect you of missing a trick. Except perhaps the most important one of all.

HUGO

And what might that be?

CARLOTTA

The knack of discovering the best in people's characters instead of the worst.

HUGO

Without wishing to undermine your radiant self-confidence I must break it to you that that has been said often before. Usually by ardent lady journalists.

CARLOTTA

One two—one two—and through and through—the vorpal blade went snicker-snack.

HUGO

My dear Carlotta. I had no idea you had such a thorough grounding in the classics. You were virtually illiterate when we first met.

CARLOTTA
(*laughing*)

It was you who set my stumbling feet upon the path of literature, Hugo. It was you who opened my eyes to many wonders.

43

HUGO

Don't talk such nonsense.

CARLOTTA

You worked assiduously on my virgin mind. And now I come to think of it you didn't do so badly with my virgin body.

HUGO
(*turning away*)
Please don't talk like that, Carlotta. I find it distasteful.

CARLOTTA
(*gently*)
Try not to be so easily cross with me. It's almost too reminiscent. You always told me I was vulgar. According to your lights that is. But your lights are so bright and highly placed that they bring out the bags under my eyes and the guttersnipe in my character. They always did and they always will. There's really nothing I can do about it, except perhaps go away. Would you like me to go away, now, this very minute? I promise I will if you truly want me to. You don't even have to answer. A valedictory little nod will be enough.

HUGO

Of course I don't want you to go away. With all my faults and in spite of my "jaundiced" view of my fellow creatures, I am seldom discourteous.

CARLOTTA

I would like it to be something warmer than your courtesy that wishes me to stay.

HUGO

I fear I can offer you little more at the moment, Carlotta, except perhaps curiosity, which is even less complimentary. I have

44

reached a stage in life when sudden surprises stimulate me less
agreeably than they might have done in my earlier years. I am
what is called "set in my ways" which at my age is not entirely to
be wondered at.

CARLOTTA

It implies resignation.

HUGO

Resignation has much to recommend it. Dignity for one thing, a
quality, alas, that is fast disappearing from our world.

CARLOTTA

I think I know what you're up to.

HUGO

(*still secure on Olympus*)

I am open to any suggestions.

CARLOTTA

You are remodelling your public image. The witty, cynical author
of so many best sellers is making way for the Grand Old Man of
Letters.

HUGO

Supposing your surmise to be accurate, do you consider such a
transition reprehensible?

CARLOTTA

Of course not, if the process is inevitable and necessary. But
aren't you jumping the gun a little?

HUGO

(*patiently*)

No, Carlotta. I am not jumping the gun, or grasping Time by the
forelock, or rushing my fences.

45

CARLOTTA

You must be prepared for a few clichés if you invite retired actresses to dinner.

HUGO

(*ignoring her interruption*)

I am merely accepting, without undue dismay, the fact of my own mortality. I am an old man and *I* at least have the sense to realise it.

CARLOTTA

Don't be waspish, my dear. Just as we are getting along so nicely. At least you can congratulate yourself, on having had a fabulously successful career. How wonderful to have been able to entertain and amuse so many millions of people for such a long time. No wonder you got a Knighthood.

HUGO

I begin to suspect that you are here as an enemy. I hoped for a friend.

CARLOTTA

Did you, Hugo? Did you really?

HUGO

Perhaps I was wrong?

CARLOTTA

No. You were not wrong. I think I am more friend than foe, but I suppose there must still be a little bitterness left. After all we were lovers once, for two whole years actually. Our parting was not very happy, was it?

HUGO

Fairly inevitable at any rate.

46

CARLOTTA

I really was very much in love with you.

HUGO

And I with you.

CARLOTTA

How convincingly you said that.

HUGO

(*turning away irritably*)

Oh really, Carlotta! Shall we stop sorting out our dead emotions now? I dislike looking at faded photographs.

CARLOTTA

Why did you write so unkindly about me in your memoirs?

HUGO

Aha! Now I'm beginning to understand.

CARLOTTA

(*cheerfully*)

Oh no you're not. You're merely jumping to conclusions. That was always one of your most glaring defects.

HUGO

Why can't we concentrate for a moment on some of my glaring assets? It might lighten the atmosphere.

CARLOTTA

We will, when you've answered my question.

HUGO

My autobiography was the assessment of the events and experiences of my life up to the date of writing it. I endeavoured to be as objective and truthful as possible. If in the process I happened to hurt your feelings, I apologise. There was no unkindness intended. I merely wrote what I thought to be true.

CARLOTTA

Your book may have been an assessment of the *outward* experiences of your life, but I cannot feel that you were entirely honest about your inner ones.

HUGO

Why should I be? My inner feelings are my own affair.

CARLOTTA

In that case the book was sailing under false colours.

HUGO

(*nastily*)

And all this because I described you as a mediocre actress.

CARLOTTA

(*laughing*)

Did you really say that? I'd forgotten. How catty of you.

HUGO

I've already said I was sorry.

CARLOTTA

No, my dear. You apologised. It isn't quite the same thing.

HUGO

(*a little guilty*)

I'm sorry then. There—will that do?

CARLOTTA

Yes. That will do for the moment. Are you working on anything now?

HUGO

Yes, a novel. Unfortunately I have been a little ill lately which halted progress for a time, but now I am back again to more or less my normal routine.

CARLOTTA

Your self-discipline was always remarkable.

HUGO

It was less constant when we knew each other. (*he smiles*) There were too many distractions.

CARLOTTA

Did you think I was a mediocre actress then?

HUGO

How could I? I was in love with you.

CARLOTTA

It was later, when you laid aside your rose-coloured glasses, that you saw through me?

HUGO

It isn't exactly that I saw through you. It was that I realised that, in spite of your vitality and charm and outward "allure," there was some essential quality missing.

CARLOTTA

You mean you guessed that I would never really become a star?

HUGO

I sensed it rather than guessed it.

CARLOTTA

Anyway your diagnosis was accurate. I never did become a star, a real star, but my career hasn't been altogether a failure, you know.

49

I've played interesting plays and travelled the wide world. My life has fascinated and amused me all along the line. I'm seldom bored and I have few regrets.

HUGO

But the one abiding one is that you would rather have been great than merely competent.

CARLOTTA
(*serenely*)

You don't happen to have any parchment lying about, do you?

HUGO

Parchment?

CARLOTTA

Yes. When zoological experts extract the venom from snakes they force them to bite on parchment.

HUGO
(*with a thin smile*)

I accept your rebuke.

CARLOTTA

How generous of you.

HUGO

It's curious that you should still be able to arouse hostility in me.

CARLOTTA

Not really. As a matter of fact it was always there, just below the surface.

HUGO

When two young people are passionately in love, a certain amount of bickering is inevitable. It even has charm, up to a point. But when the old indulge in it, it is merely tiresome.

CARLOTTA

Speak for yourself. You are the one who has decided to be old. I haven't yet, maybe I never shall. Some people remain young until they're ninety.

HUGO

You see no point in dignified withdrawal, in "growing old gracefully"?

CARLOTTA

There is little grace in growing old, Hugo. It's a dreary process that we all have to deal with in our different ways. To outside observers my way may seem stupid and garish and, later on perhaps, even grotesque. But the opinion of outside observers has never troubled me unduly. I am really only accountable to myself. I like slapping on the make-up and having my body massaged and my hair tinted. You've no idea how much I enjoy my long, complicated mornings. I admit I'm liable to cave in a bit by the late afternoon, but a short snooze fixes that and then I have all the fun of getting ready again for the evening.

HUGO

And does the evening really justify so much effort?

CARLOTTA

As a general rule, yes. I have many friends, some of them quite young. They seem to enjoy my company. I like to watch them dancing.

HUGO

I detest the young of today. They are grubby, undisciplined, and ill-mannered. They also make too much noise.

CARLOTTA

Youth always makes too much noise. Many of the ones I know
are better informed and more intelligent than we were. Also their
world is more shrill than ours was. You really must make allowances.

HUGO

I'm too old to make allowances.

CARLOTTA

Oh Hugo! You're positively stampeding towards the quiet grave,
aren't you?

HUGO

Shall we change the subject? Shall we try to discover some general
theme on which we can both agree?

CARLOTTA

Your indestructible elegance is flustering me and making me talk
too much.

HUGO
(without malice)

You always talked too much, Carlotta.

CARLOTTA

Ah yes. It's a compulsive disease. Useful at dinner parties but fatal
in the home.

HUGO

As this is neither, you can afford to relax.

CARLOTTA

There's so much I want to know about you, about what's happened to you during these long years, and here I am talking you
into the ground. Will you forgive me?

HUGO

Why is there so much that you want to know about me? Why are you so suddenly curious about what has happened to me during these long years? Some motive must have impelled you to come here, some spark must have been struck. What was it?

CARLOTTA

All in good time.

HUGO

I think you will agree that that is an extremely exasperating reply.

CARLOTTA

Yes it is, isn't it? Again I must ask you to forgive me.

HUGO

If our first evening together after so many years is to be devoted entirely to mutual apologies, it may become tedious.

CARLOTTA

I think I can guarantee that whatever the evening may become it will not be tedious.

HUGO

Do I detect an undercurrent of menace? Is it in your mind to revive our dead and forgotten sex duel?

CARLOTTA

Is that how you remember it? How sad.

HUGO

Carlotta! What is it that you want of me?

CARLOTTA

At the moment, dinner.

53

HUGO

(*with irritation*)

Carlotta!

CARLOTTA

I only had a salad for lunch and I'm famished.

HUGO

(*resigned*)

Very well. Have it your own way. I am prepared to play any game you wish to play, up to a point. But do remember, won't you, that I tire easily. (*He rings the bell*) The dinner is ordered anyhow. I even remembered that you liked caviar.

CARLOTTA

That was sweet of you. The first time I ever tasted it was with you. You took me to Ciro's for supper after the show.

HUGO

Was I still wooing you then, or had I won?

CARLOTTA

You'd already won, more or less, but I think the caviar clinched it. I can remember what we had after the caviar too.

HUGO

What was it?

CARLOTTA

A filet mignon with sauce Bearnaise and a green salad and the . . . (*She thinks for a moment*) Then a chocolate soufflé.

HUGO

Did we by any chance have pink champagne as well?

CARLOTTA

Yes. I believe we did.

HUGO

You will see in a moment with what nostalgic charm history can repeat itself.

CARLOTTA

I don't believe you're really old at all.
(*There is a knock at the door.*)

HUGO

Avanti.
(FELIX *wheels in the dinner table.*)

FELIX

Good evening, madame.

CARLOTTA

Good evening.

FELIX
(*as he comes in*)
The table in the usual place, sir?

HUGO

Yes please, Felix.

FELIX
(*seating* CARLOTTA *at the table*)
Madame.

CARLOTTA

Thank you.
(FELIX *goes to open vodka.*)

55

HUGO

You can leave the vodka, we will serve ourselves.

FELIX

Bien, monsieur. (He gives a quick glance at the table to see that everything is all right, then, with a bow, goes out of the room)

CARLOTTA

How handsome he is, isn't he? Greek or Italian?

HUGO
(pouring out vodka for them both)
Half Italian and half Austrian, I believe.

CARLOTTA

He has just a slight look of my first husband, Peter. Poor Peter. His feet trod the world lightly, and alas, all too briefly.

HUGO

He was the one who was killed in an aeroplane?

CARLOTTA

Yes. He was studying to be a pilot in San Diego. I was trying out a new play in San Francisco. They had the sense not to tell me until after the matinée.

HUGO
(a little embarrassed by tragedy)
How dreadful for you.

CARLOTTA

Yes. It was my first real sorrow. We'd only been married for eighteen months, too soon for the gold to rub away. Then a little while afterwards I had a miscarriage. That was my second real sorrow. It was quite a year. San Francisco is a divine city and I love it, but I always seem to have bad luck when I play there. In 1957 I lost my last remaining tooth in the Curran Theatre.

HUGO
(*with a shudder of distaste*)
Carlotta!

CARLOTTA
It was a gallant old stump that held my lower plate together. I remember saying to my understudy one day, "Sally, when this is out, you're on!" And sure enough, a week later, it was and she was.

HUGO
I don't wish to sound fussy, Carlotta, but I really don't care to discuss false teeth during dinner.

CARLOTTA
(*cheerfully*)
Why ever not? That's when they're a force most to be reckoned with.

HUGO
Nevertheless, I should welcome a change of subject.

CARLOTTA
Dear Hugo. I am so sorry. I remember now, you always hated spades being called spades. What shall we talk about? Perhaps you would like some further vignettes from my rather ramshackle career?

HUGO
Provided that they are general rather than clinical.

CARLOTTA

Well let me see now. I married my second husband, Vernon Ritchie, in the spring of 1939. He was my leading man in a ghastly play about the Deep South which ran for ages.

HUGO

(*without much interest*)

Was he a good actor?

CARLOTTA

No, terrible. But he made up for his performances on the stage by his performances in—(*she hesitates*)—in the boudoir. I didn't say bed in order to spare your feelings.

HUGO

Thank you. I appreciate your delicacy.

CARLOTTA

He was a sweet man and I was very fond of him. He was the father of my son David and then, soon after Pearl Harbor when the war came to us in America, he joined the Navy and was killed in the Pacific in 1944.

HUGO

Was that another "great sorrow"?

CARLOTTA

No. Just a sadness.

HUGO

What decided you to make your life in America rather than in Europe where you were born?

CARLOTTA

Because I happened to be there I suppose. I went there originally

58

on account of you. It was your play, if you remember, that first deposited me on the Great White Way, where it ran exactly ten days.

HUGO
(*loftily*)

That was no surprise to me. I never thought they'd understand it.

CARLOTTA

Do you know, Hugo? I have a terrible feeling that they did.

HUGO

Let me help you to some more caviar.

CARLOTTA

Thank you.

HUGO
(*serving her and himself*)

And your third husband?

CARLOTTA

Dear old Spike.

HUGO

Dear old what?

CARLOTTA

Spike. Spike Frost. Lots of people are called Spike in America. As I told you he's a movie agent, and a very successful one too. He handles a lot of the big stars.

HUGO

That sounds vaguely pornographic.

CARLOTTA

(*delighted*)

Hurray! A little joke at last. Almost an off colour little joke too. Things are looking up.

HUGO

And you've never appeared in the London theatre since, since my first play?

CARLOTTA

Oh yes, twice.

HUGO

I don't remember hearing about it.

CARLOTTA

Why should you? As a matter of fact on each occasion you were away, in the Far East I believe, on one of your excavating expeditions.

HUGO

Excavating expeditions?

CARLOTTA

Yes, digging for treasure trove in the trusting minds of the innocent.

HUGO

You have a malicious tongue, Carlotta.

CARLOTTA

Yes. I really should learn to keep it between my false teeth. Let's stop talking about me now. Tell me about Hilde.

HUGO

I really see no reason to discuss Hilde with you.

CARLOTTA

Your loyal reticence does you credit, but it is a little overdone, almost defensive. After all I'm not a newspaper reporter.

HUGO

You might easily be, judging by the tastelessness of some of your questions.

CARLOTTA

It's no use trying to intimidate me, Hugo, because it won't work. If you remember it never did work. You have asked me questions about my husbands and I didn't snap your head off. Why shouldn't I ask you about your wife?

HUGO

The analogy is a trifle strained.

CARLOTTA

I truly want to know, not from idle curiosity, but because I liked her. She has wisdom and repose and her eyes are kind, a little sad perhaps, but kind. I suspect tragedy in her life.

HUGO
(giving in)

There *was* a tragedy in her life. She managed to escape from Nazi Germany in 1940, soon after the "phoney" war began. She left the love of her life behind, a young poet called Gerhardt Hendl. He died two years later in a concentration camp. Now are you satisfied?

CARLOTTA

Satisfied is not quite the word I would have chosen. But I am pleased that you told me.

(FELIX *comes in wheeling a table on which are the covered dishes for the next course.*)

61

FELIX

Am I too early, sir?

HUGO

No, we have finished. You'd better open the wine.

FELIX

Bien, monsieur.

CARLOTTA

Champagne! Oh Hugo, I have a feeling that it is going to be pink.

HUGO

It is.

CARLOTTA

How disarming of you to be so sentimental. It must be that evanescent nostalgia. Do you remember the cottage at Taplow and driving down together on summer nights after the show?

HUGO

Yes. Yes, I remember.

CARLOTTA

And how cross you were that night at the Grafton Galleries, when I appeared in a red sequin frock that Baby Briant had lent me. You said I looked like a Shaftesbury Avenue tart.

HUGO

You did.

(FELIX, *having cleared away the first course and opened the bottle of champagne, pours a little into* HUGO's *glass.* HUGO *sips it and nods his approval.* FELIX *then fills both their glasses and proceeds to serve the filets mignon, salad, etc.*)

CARLOTTA

And the weekend we went to Paris, and I got back to the theatre
on the Monday night exactly seven minutes before curtain time.
My understudy was all dressed and ready to go on . . . I often
wonder why you didn't write any more plays. Your dialogue was
so pointed and witty.

HUGO

You flatter me, Carlotta.

CARLOTTA

I've read everything you've ever written.

HUGO

You flatter me more than ever.

CARLOTTA

I only said that I'd read everything you've ever written. I ventured
no opinion, flattering or otherwise.

HUGO

The statement alone is flattering enough.

CARLOTTA

Yes. Yes, I expect it is. I suppose Ciro's isn't there any more?
(*She sighs*) Oh, dear!

HUGO

That was a pensive sigh.

CARLOTTA

I've been in America too long. It's so lovely to see a steak that
doesn't look like a bedroom slipper . . .

FELIX
(*having finished serving*)
Tout va bien monsieur?

HUGO
Oui, excellent. Merci, Felix.

FELIX
A *votre service, monsieur*. (*He bows and leaves the room*)

CARLOTTA
He really is most attractive, isn't he? Those glorious shoulders.

HUGO
I've never noticed them.

CARLOTTA
They're probably padded anyhow. Life can be dreadfully treacherous.

HUGO
(*he laughs quite genuinely*)
You really are extraordinary, Carlotta. You don't look a day over fifty.

CARLOTTA
I should hope not. After three cellular injections and two facelifts.

HUGO
(*pained*)
Carlotta!

CARLOTTA
It's wonderful how they do it now. You can hardly see the scars at all.

64

HUGO

What on earth possessed you to tell me that?

CARLOTTA

Oh dear. Now I've shocked you again.

HUGO

Aesthetically yes, you have.

CARLOTTA

I am sorry. Just as we were making such progress.

HUGO

As the object of such operations is, presumably, to create an illusion, why destroy the illusion by telling everybody about it?

CARLOTTA

Quite right, Hugo. As a matter of fact you could do with a little snip yourself. Just under the chin.

HUGO

I wouldn't dream of it.

CARLOTTA

It would do wonders for your morale.

HUGO

My morale is perfectly satisfactory as it is, thank you.

CARLOTTA
(gaily)

Long may it remain so.

HUGO
(after a slight pause)

Why did you come here, Carlotta?

65

CARLOTTA

I told you. I'm having a course of injections at Professor Boromelli's clinique.

HUGO

(*frowning*)

Professor Boromelli!

CARLOTTA

Yes. Do you know him?

HUGO

I know of him.

CARLOTTA

You look disapproving.

HUGO

His reputation is rather dubious.

CARLOTTA

In what way?

HUGO

The general concensus of opinion is that he's a quack.

CARLOTTA

Quack or no quack he's an old duck.

HUGO

Don't be foolish, Carlotta.

CARLOTTA

There's no need to stamp on my little joke as though it were a cockroach.

66

HUGO

Well? (*He smiles a faintly strained smile*) I'm still waiting to hear the reason that induced you suddenly to make this, shall we say, rather tardy reappearance in my life? It must be a fairly strong one.

CARLOTTA

Not so very strong really. It's only actually an irrelevant little favour. Irrelevant to you I mean, but important to me.

HUGO

What is it?

CARLOTTA

Prepare yourself for a tiny shock.

HUGO
(*with a note of impatience*)

I'm quite prepared. Go on.

CARLOTTA

I too have written an autobiography.

HUGO
(*raising his eyebrows*)

Have you? How interesting.

CARLOTTA

There's a distinct chill in your voice.

HUGO

I'm sorry. I was unaware of it.

CARLOTTA

It is to be published in the autumn.

HUGO

Congratulations. Who by?

CARLOTTA

Doubleday in New York and Heinemann in London.

HUGO
(*concealing surprise*)

Excellent.

CARLOTTA
(*with a trace of irony*)

I am so glad you approve.

HUGO

And have you written it all yourself? Or have you employed what
I believe is described as a "ghost writer"?

CARLOTTA

No, Hugo. I have written every word of it myself.

HUGO

Well done.

CARLOTTA

On an electric typewriter. You really should try one. It's a god-
send.

HUGO

I have no need of it. Hilde does my typing for me.

CARLOTTA

Of course, yes—I'd forgotten. Then you can give her one for a
birthday present.

68

HUGO

(*after a slight pause*)

I suppose you want me to write an introductory preface.

CARLOTTA

No. I've already done that myself.

HUGO

(*with a tinge of irritation*)

What is it then? What is it that you want of me?

CARLOTTA

Permission to publish your letters.

HUGO

(*startled*)

Letters! What letters?

CARLOTTA

The letters you wrote to me when we were lovers. I've kept them all.

HUGO

Whatever letters I wrote to you at that time were private. They concerned no one but you and me.

CARLOTTA

I agree. But that was a long time ago. Before we'd either of us become celebrated enough to write our memoirs.

HUGO

I cannot feel that you, Carlotta, have even yet achieved that particular distinction.

CARLOTTA

(*unruffled*)

Doubleday and Heinemann do.

HUGO

I believe that some years ago Mrs. Patrick Campbell made a similar request to Mr. George Bernard Shaw and his reply was, "Certainly not. I have no intention of playing the horse to your Lady Godiva."

CARLOTTA

How unkind.

HUGO

It would ill become me to attempt to improve on Mr. George Bernard Shaw.

CARLOTTA

(*helping herself to some more salad*)

You mean you refuse?

HUGO

Certainly. I most emphatically refuse.

CARLOTTA

I thought you would.

HUGO

In that case surely it was waste of time to take the trouble to ask me?

CARLOTTA

I just took a chance. After all, life can be full of surprises sometimes, can't it?

70

HUGO

If your forthcoming autobiography is to be peppered with that sort of bromide it cannot fail to achieve the best seller list.

CARLOTTA

You can turn nasty quickly, can't you? You were quite cosy and relaxed a moment ago.

HUGO

I am completely horrified by your suggestion. It's in the worst possible taste.

CARLOTTA

Never mind. Let's have some more champagne. (*She takes the bottle out of the bucket and pours herself some. She holds it up to him enquiringly*)

HUGO

Not for me, thank you.

CARLOTTA

There's quite a lot left.

HUGO

Finish it by all means.

CARLOTTA

Professor Boromelli will be furious.

HUGO

I gather he doesn't insist on any particular regime. What sort of injections does he give you?

CARLOTTA
(*enjoying her steak*)
Oh it's a formula of his own. Hormones and things.

71

HUGO

The same kind of treatment as Niehans?

CARLOTTA

Oh no, quite different. Niehans injects living cells from an unborn ewe, and as long as he doesn't pick a non U Ewe it works like a charm.

HUGO

Have you been to him as well?

CARLOTTA

Oh yes, ages ago. He's an old duck too.

HUGO

You seem to regard Switzerland as a sort of barnyard.

CARLOTTA
(*raising her glass to him*)

Quack quack!

HUGO
(*crossly*)

Don't be so childish.

CARLOTTA
(*laughing*)

You used to enjoy my jokes when you and I were young love and all the world was new.

HUGO

Flippancy in a girl of twenty-one can be quite attractive, in a woman of more mature years it is liable to be embarrassing.

CARLOTTA

Like bad temper in a pompous old gentleman.

(FELIX *re-enters, wheeling a table on which is a chocolate soufflé.*)

Perfect timing, Felix. I congratulate you.

FELIX

Thank you, madame. (*He deftly removes the empty plates, places them on the movable table, places clean ones before them and proceeds to serve the soufflé*)

CARLOTTA
(*after a longish pause*)

The lake's like glass tonight. There'll be a moon presently.

HUGO

How clever of you to know.

CARLOTTA

There was a moon last night. I just put two and two together. (*to* FELIX) Sir Hugo tells me you are half Austrian and half Italian, Felix.

FELIX

That is correct, madame.

CARLOTTA

Which half do you like best?

HUGO

Please, Carlotta . . .

FELIX

I find the two perfectly satisfactory, madame. (*He smiles*)

CARLOTTA

I expect both the waltz and the tarantella come quite naturally to you.

HUGO

(*testily*)

That will be all for the moment, Felix. Please bring the coffee immediately.

FELIX

Subito signore! (*He bows, smiles at* CARLOTTA, *and leaves*)

HUGO

I hate familiarity with servants.

CARLOTTA

Oh eat up your soufflé for God's sake and stop being so disagreeable.

HUGO

(*outraged*)

How dare you speak to me like that!

CARLOTTA

Dare? Really, Hugo. What have I to fear from you?

HUGO

I consider your rudeness insufferable.

CARLOTTA

And I consider your pomposity insufferable.

HUGO

(*icily*)

I should like to remind you that you are my guest.

CARLOTTA

Of course I am. Don't be so silly.

74

HUGO

And as such I have the right to demand from you at least a semblance of good manners.

CARLOTTA

"Semblance of good manners"! Talk about clichés. That's a clanger if ever I heard one.

HUGO
(*quivering with rage*)

Once and for all, Carlotta . . .

CARLOTTA

For heaven's sake, calm down. Your wife told me earlier on that it was bad for you to overexcite yourself. You'll have a fit in a minute if you don't stop gibbering.

HUGO
(*beside himself, shouting*)

I am not gibbering!
(*There is a silence for a moment.* CARLOTTA *continues to eat her soufflé.* HUGO *rises majestically.*)

HUGO
(*with superb control*)

I think, Carlotta, that as we really haven't very much more to say to each other, it would be considerate of you to leave as soon as you've finished eating. As I told you, I have been rather ill recently and it is my habit to retire early. I also feel that I have reached an age when I no longer have to tolerate being spoken to as you spoke just now.

CARLOTTA

If you are determined to decline so rapidly you'll soon reach an age when nobody will be able to speak to you at all.

75

HUGO

I am sorry if I appear to be discourteous but after all, it was you
who forced us both into this—this rather unprofitable meeting.
I have done my best to receive you kindly and make the evening
a pleasant one. That I have failed is only too obvious. I am sorry
also that I was unable to accede to your request. I am sure, after
you have given yourself time to think it over, that you will realise
how impertinent it was.

CARLOTTA

Why impertinent?

HUGO

Not having read your book I have naturally no way of judging
whether it is good, bad, or indifferent. I am perfectly aware however, that whatever its merits, the inclusion of private letters from
a man in my position, would enhance its value considerably. The
impertinence I think lies in your assuming for a moment that I
should grant you permission to publish them. We met and parted
many years ago. Since then we have neither of us communicated
with each other. You have pursued your career, I have pursued
mine. Mine, if I may say so without undue arrogance, has been
eminently successful. Yours, perhaps less so. Doesn't it strike *you*
as impertinent that, after so long a silence, you should suddenly
ask me to provide you with my name as a steppingstone?

CARLOTTA
(*looking at him thoughtfully*)
Am I to be allowed a cup of coffee before I leave?

HUGO

Of course. He will bring it in a moment.

CARLOTTA

Poor Hugo.

76

HUGO

I am in no need of your commiseration.

CARLOTTA

Think carefully and you may not be quite so sure.

HUGO

I haven't the faintest idea what you are implying nor, I must frankly admit, am I particularly interested.

CARLOTTA

I am implying that a man who is capable of refusing a request as gracelessly and contemptuously as you have done can be neither happy nor secure.

HUGO

Happy and secure? My dear Carlotta, I salute the facility with which you have picked up the glib, sentimental jargon of American women's magazines.

CARLOTTA

Look out, Hugo. You are riding for a fall. Your high horse may suddenly buck and throw you.

(FELIX *enters with the coffee.*)

FELIX

Coffee, monsieur?

HUGO

For Madame only. You can put it over here and take away the dinner table.

FELIX

Very good, sir.

CARLOTTA

You are afraid of not sleeping?

HUGO

(*coldly*)

I never drink coffee in the evening.

CARLOTTA

What about a nice cup of cocoa? Inelegant but soothing.

FELIX

That will be all, monsieur?

HUGO

Yes, thank you.

FELIX

Good night, sir, madame.

CARLOTTA

Good night Felix. The dinner was delicious and the service impeccable.

FELIX

(*shooting a quizzical glance at* HUGO's *stony face*)

Madame is most kind. A *votre service, monsieur.* (*He bows and wheels the table out of the room*)

HUGO

(*pouring out a cup of coffee*)

Do you take sugar?

CARLOTTA

Yes please, a little. How long have I got before the curfew sounds?

78

HUGO

(ignoring this)

Here's your coffee.

CARLOTTA

The letters really are very good, Hugo. It's disappointing that you won't allow me to use them. They *are* love letters of course up to a point and brilliantly written. The more ardent passages are exquisitely phrased although they do give the impression that they were commissioned by your head rather than dictated by your heart.

HUGO

I have no wish to discuss the matter any further.

CARLOTTA

It seems a pity that posterity should be deprived of such an illuminating example of your earlier work.

HUGO

I really am very tired, Carlotta. I feel that my age entitles me to ask you to leave me alone now. Perhaps we may meet and talk again within the next few days.

CARLOTTA

My wrap is in your bedroom. Hilde put it there. May I fetch it?

HUGO

By all means.

(CARLOTTA *goes into the bedroom.* HUGO *lights a cigarette and then immediately stubs it out again. He is obviously seething with irritation. He opens the table drawer, takes two white tablets out of a bottle and crunches them.* CARLOTTA *returns.*)

79

CARLOTTA

Good night, Hugo. I am sorry the evening has ended so, so uncosily.

HUGO

So am I, Carlotta. So am I.

CARLOTTA

(*turning, on her way to the door*)

To revert for a moment to the unfortunate subject of the letters. You may have them if you like. They are of no further use to me.

HUGO

That is most generous of you.

CARLOTTA

I'm afraid I can't let you have the others though. That would be betraying a sacred promise.

HUGO

Others? What others?

CARLOTTA

Your letters to Perry.

HUGO

(*visibly shaken*)

My letters to Perry! What do you mean?

CARLOTTA

Perry Sheldon. I happened to be with him when he died.

HUGO

What do you know about Perry Sheldon?

CARLOTTA

Among other things that he was the only true love of your life.
Good night, Hugo. Sleep well.

Curtain as CARLOTTA *turns upstage exiting through the door.*

ACT II

TIME: *A few minutes later.*

When the curtain rises HUGO *is sitting in his armchair staring into space. Finally, with an effort, he rises, goes over to the drink table, and pours out a glass of brandy. He drinks it in one gulp. He walks over to the window and back again several times. At last, having made his decision, he goes to the telephone.*

HUGO
(at telephone)

'Allo—Gaston? *Je veux parler avec Madame Gray, Madame Carlotta Gray. Oui, elle est arrivée cet apres-midi* . . . *Merci, j'attendrai. (he waits)* Hallo—Carlotta? Yes it's I, Hugo . . . Don't pretend to be surprised. Quite a lot is the matter and you know it . . . Will you please come back. I must talk to you. Please, Carlotta . . . No, you know perfectly well that it can't wait until tomorrow. You've won your point, for God's sake have the grace not to exult too much. Please come . . . Yes now—immediately. Very well. Thank you, Carlotta.

(He hangs up the telephone and sits for a moment with his head buried in his hands. Then he gets up, goes slowly over to the table, takes a cigarette, lights it and resumes his pacing of the room. There is little energy in his movements. He is a worried, unhappy man. Presently there is a perfunctory knock on the door and CARLOTTA *comes in. He stops his pacing and they stand looking at each other in silence for a moment.)*

CARLOTTA
(with the ghost of a smile)

I'm sorry, Hugo. That was an unkind trick. But you had it coming to you.

HUGO

I would like, if you don't mind, a little further explanation of what
you said when you left me a few minutes ago.

CARLOTTA

Shall we sit down? It looks rather foolish standing here and sizing
each other up like a couple of Japanese wrestlers.

HUGO

I have no wrestling match in mind, Oriental or otherwise. I have
already admitted defeat. (*He motions her to a chair*)

CARLOTTA

(*sitting down*)

Oh no you haven't, Hugo. Not quite yet. But there's no hurry.
Oh by the way, I met that charming Felix in the corridor and
ordered another bottle of champagne. I do hope you don't mind.
I thought we might need it.

HUGO

I see you have decided to set the mood in a light vein.

CARLOTTA

You are the challenged. You have the choice of weapons. We can
send the champagne away again if you like.

(*There is a knock on the door and* FELIX *enters carrying a
bottle of champagne in a bucket of ice and two glasses.*)

FELIX

The champagne, monsieur.

HUGO

Thank you, Felix. You may put it on the table.

FELIX

Would you wish me to open it?

83

CARLOTTA

Please do, Felix. I am sure that neither Sir Hugo nor I could manage it as efficiently as you.

FELIX

Certainement, madame. (*He proceeds to open the bottle*)

CARLOTTA

I was right about the moon. Look, Hugo. It's making a path right across the lake. How sad for you, Felix, to have to rush about serving people in this stuffy hotel when you might be dancing your heart away in one of those little open-air cafes on the shore.

FELIX

There is time for everything, madame.

CARLOTTA

But not for everybody, Felix. Not for everybody.
(FELIX, *having opened the bottle and filled two glasses, brings one to* CARLOTTA.)

FELIX

Madame.

CARLOTTA
(*taking it*)

Thank you, Felix.

FELIX
(*taking the other glass to* HUGO)

Monsieur.

HUGO

Put it down, please. I will drink it later.

FELIX

(*obeying*)

That will be all, monsieur?

HUGO

(*irritably*)

Yes, yes—that will be all, good night.

FELIX

(*to* CARLOTTA)

I have put a bottle of Evian in your room, madame, as you requested.

CARLOTTA

Thank you, Felix. Good night.

FELIX

Good night, madame. (*He bows and goes*)

CARLOTTA

Well I must say it's pleasant to have *one* request granted, even if it's only a bottle of Evian.

HUGO

I am finding the flippancy of your manner extremely irritating.

CARLOTTA

Now that I come to think of it, you always did. In any case this is not a tragic situation, Hugo. All the tragedy was drained out of it when poor Perry died. There's only comedy left now. Rather bitter comedy, I admit, but not entirely unenjoyable.

HUGO

You must forgive my lack of humour.

CARLOTTA

You never had much anyhow. Wit, yes, a brilliant talent for the sharp riposte, the swift, malicious phrase. But true humour lies in the capacity to laugh at oneself. That you could never do.

HUGO

I fear it is a little too late for me to change.

CARLOTTA

Ah yes. Much too late. It's all too late now. That's the pity of it. I should have sought you out before. Who knows? I might have been able to do a little good.

HUGO

If you had, would blackmail have so strongly coloured your missionary zeal?

CARLOTTA

Blackmail? Really, Hugo! I had no idea you had such a highly developed sense of melodrama.

HUGO

You said you were with Perry Sheldon when he died. Is that true?

CARLOTTA

Yes. (*She takes a sip of champagne*)

HUGO

And you have in your possession letters written by me to him?

CARLOTTA

Yes. Love letters most of them. They are less meticulously lyrical than the ones you wrote to me, but there is more genuine feeling in them. They were written in your earlier years, remember, before your mind had become corrupted by fame and your heart by caution. The last ones were written in the last years of his life. There are three of them. All refusals to help him when he was in desperate straits. They also are fascinating in their way, masterpieces of veiled invective. Pure gold for your future biographer.

HUGO

(*controlling a quiver in his voice*)
Did you steal these letters?

CARLOTTA

No, Hugo. I didn't steal them. He gave them to me three days before he died.

HUGO

What do you propose to do with them?

CARLOTTA

I haven't quite decided yet. I made him a promise.

HUGO

What sort of promise?

CARLOTTA

I promised him that if he gave them to me I would keep them safe until the time came when they could be used to the best advantage.

HUGO

Used? To the best advantage! Used in what way?

CARLOTTA

By a suitable biographer.

HUGO

And are you intending to be that biographer?

CARLOTTA

Oh no. I am not experienced enough. It would require someone more detached and objective than I am to write an accurate and unbiased account of you. My personal feelings would be involved.

HUGO

Your personal feelings would still be involved after more than half a lifetime?

CARLOTTA

Memory is curiously implacable. It can forget joy but it seldom forgets humiliation.

HUGO

Your emotional tenacity is remarkable.

CARLOTTA

There is no longer any emotion in my feelings for you, Hugo.

HUGO

Wouldn't you consider revenge an emotion?

CARLOTTA
(*with a little laugh*)
Revenge! You're jumping to the wrong conclusions again.

HUGO

I wouldn't expect you to admit it.

CARLOTTA

You're wrong. I'd admit it like a shot if it were true, but it isn't. As a matter of fact my motives in all this are altruistic rather than vindictive. Suddenly, in my raddled old age I have seen the light. I find myself obsessed with a desire to right wrongs, to see justice done, to snatch a brand from the burning.

88

HUGO

I am not impressed.

CARLOTTA

Never mind. The night is young.

HUGO

To revert to the subject of my, as yet unnamed, biographer. Have you found one?

CARLOTTA

Of course.

HUGO

(*still with admirable calm*)

May I ask his name?

CARLOTTA

Certainly. His name is Justin Chandler. He used to be a professor at Harvard. I met him first when I was playing *Hedda Gabler* in Boston.

HUGO

(*fury breaking through*)

I don't give a damn what you were playing in Boston.

CARLOTTA

I know you don't, but it was *Hedda Gabler*.

HUGO

Am I to believe that this eminent Harvard professor is contemplating writing a biography of me without even asking my permission?

CARLOTTA

He'll probably get round to that later when he has completed his notes. He's been planning it for years. He's always been a fan of yours.

HUGO

Has he indeed.

CARLOTTA

He once wrote a monograph on you for the *Atlantic Monthly*. It was called "Technique and What Next?". He is a fervent admirer of your literary craftsmanship. He said that your autobiography was the most superlative example of sustained camouflage that he had ever read. He certainly is a smart cookie.

HUGO

My knowledge of American slang is limited.

CARLOTTA

The exact English translation would be clever biscuit.

HUGO

And is it your intention to hand over to this—this "clever biscuit" private letters of mine which were written to somebody else over thirty years ago?

CARLOTTA

You must realise that they are exceedingly valuable documents. Your fame has made them so. Not only financially valuable, although I have no doubt that they'd fetch quite a fancy price at a public auction, but their importance to anyone who wishes to make an analytical survey of your life and career, is too obvious to be ignored. Owing to your own ceaseless vigilance your "bubble reputation" must be almost as solid as a football by now. You mustn't be surprised that certain people should wish to kick it about a bit.

HUGO

How much do you want?

CARLOTTA

Don't be *silly*, Hugo. Give me a little more champagne. I suggest
that you'd better have some too while you're at it. It might help
to clear your mind.

HUGO

(*taking her glass*)

I have no alternative but to follow your lead, Carlotta. If your
object in all this is to humiliate and embarrass me, you have so
clearly succeeded that no further comment is necessary. What is
the next move? (*He fills her glass and hands it to her*)

CARLOTTA

Thank you.

HUGO

(*with an effort*)

The knowledge that my letters to Perry Sheldon are still in exist-
ence has naturally come as a considerable shock to me. It would
be foolish to deny it.

CARLOTTA

(*sipping her champagne*)

Also unconvincing.

HUGO

I presume you have taken the trouble to acquaint yourself with
the legal aspects of the situation?

CARLOTTA

The legal aspects of the situation are fairly simple. Any letter
from the moment it is posted, automatically becomes the property

of the recipient. In this case Perry was the recipient. He made the
letters over to me in a written statement which was witnessed by
a public notary. They now legally belong to me and I am at liberty
to do what I like with them.

HUGO

I fear you have been misinformed. The letters may indeed be
your property, but according to law they may not be published
without my permission or, when I die, the permission of my es-
tate.

CARLOTTA

I am sure you are right, but so far there has been no question of
them being published. The important fact is that they exist, and
for so long as they continue to exist they will remain a potential
menace to your carefully sculptured reputation.

HUGO

Where are the letters?

CARLOTTA

I have them with me.

HUGO

You have not yet told me what you propose to do with them.

CARLOTTA

Because I have not yet decided. There is still what you describe
as my "missionary zeal" to be taken into account.

HUGO

I don't know what you are talking about.

CARLOTTA

All in good time, Hugo. All in good time.

HUGO
(*losing his temper*)

This is intolerable!

CARLOTTA

Keep calm.

HUGO

I have been calm long enough. I am sick to death of this interminable witless skirmishing. Come to the point, if there is a point beyond your feline compulsion to torment me and insult me. The implications behind all the highfaluting rubbish you have been talking have not been lost on me. The veiled threat is perfectly clear.

CARLOTTA

What veiled threat?

HUGO

The threat to expose to the world the fact that I have had, in the past, homosexual tendencies.

CARLOTTA
(*calmly*)

Homosexual tendencies in the past! What nonsense! You've been a homosexual all your life, and you know it!

HUGO
(*shouting*)

That is not true!

CARLOTTA

Don't shout. It's waste of adrenalin. You've no idea what it does to the inside of your stomach when you work yourself into a state like that. If you won't drink champagne for God's sake have a

93

little brandy and pull yourself together. Here—I'll get you some.
(*She goes purposefully to the drink table*)

HUGO
(*near hysteria*)

I don't care what you do—do you hear me? You can publish whatever letters you like and be damned to you.

CARLOTTA
(*handing him a glass of brandy*)

Here Hugo. Drink this and stop being hysterical.

HUGO
(*knocking the glass out of her hand*)

Go away—go away from me—leave me alone! (*He sinks into his
chair and puts his hand over his face*)

CARLOTTA

There. Now look what you've done! Brandy stains all over that
nice rug. For shame, Hugo! You're behaving like a petulant little
boy at a children's party.

HUGO

Go away and leave me alone.

CARLOTTA

Be careful. I might take you at your word. You know perfectly
well that if I went away now and left you alone that you'd be on
the telephone within ten minutes imploring me to come back.

HUGO

I am an old man, Carlotta, and, as I already told you, I have recently been ill, very ill. I have neither the strength nor the will
to continue this, this embittered conflict that you have forced
upon me. I am too tired.

94

CARLOTTA

If I poured you out another glass of brandy, would you again dash it to the ground or would you drink it calmly and sensibly?

HUGO

I am not supposed to drink brandy. It is bad for my heart.

CARLOTTA

(*going to the drink table*)

I feel on this particular occasion a little licence might be permitted. (*She pours out another glass of brandy and brings it to him*) Here, I think that your heart, what there is of it, will survive.

HUGO

(*taking it and looking at her*)

Why do you hate me so? Is it because you once loved me?

CARLOTTA

You've got it all wrong, Hugo. I don't hate you, and loving you I only dimly remember.

HUGO

(*taking a swig of brandy*)

You underrate my intelligence.

CARLOTTA

Oh no. I may have overrated your stamina but I would never underrate your intelligence. Your intelligence is of a very high order indeed, up to a certain point. It is what happens over and above that point that arouses my curiosity.

HUGO

I don't know what you're talking about.

CARLOTTA

You flew into a fine theatrical passion just now when I said you had been homosexual all your life. Did you consider that an insult?

HUGO

Wasn't it intended to be?

CARLOTTA

Of course not. We are living in the nineteen-sixties not the eighteen-nineties.

HUGO

(nastily)

This sophisticated tolerance hardly fits in with the sneer in your voice when you accused me of it.

CARLOTTA

You are oversensitive. If there had been a sneer in my voice, which there wasn't, it would not have been a sneer at the fact, but at your lifelong repudiation of it. In any case I did not accuse you of it, for the simple reason that I do not consider it a crime. What I am accusing you of is something far worse than that. Complacent cruelty and moral cowardice.

HUGO

On what evidence?

CARLOTTA

On the evidence of every book you've ever written and the dismal record of your personal relationships.

HUGO

You know nothing of my personal relationships. We are strangers.

96

CARLOTTA

On the contrary I know a great deal about them. I've been making diligent enquiries for quite a long time. It's been rather fun, piecing together odd bits of information, talking to people you've known here and there in course of your travels. Your name is unfailing as a conversational gambit. Your ivory tower is not nearly so sacrosanct as you imagine it to be. You cannot be half so naïve as to imagine that a man of your sustained eminence could ever be entirely immune from the breath of scandal, however gingerly you may have trodden your secret paths.

HUGO

I am not interested in the scruffy surmises of the mediocre.

CARLOTTA

By no means all the people I discussed you with were mediocre, and by no means all the things I heard were surmises.

HUGO

Nor am I interested in your opinion nor anyone else's opinion of my character. What I am interested in is the motive that impelled you to come here.

CARLOTTA

I find it awfully difficult to explain even to myself. I suppose basically that it was irritation more than anything else.

HUGO
(outraged)

Irritation!

CARLOTTA

And don't minimize the force of that apparently trivial little emotion. It can be more powerful than anger and more devastating than hatred. It can wear away rocks and stones and human tissues.

97

It can also play merry hell with the kindliest of dispositions. I am not by nature a vindictive character but you have irritated me for years and I am determined to put an end to it before my whole system is poisoned.

HUGO
(with commendable calm)
It might clarify the situation for me if I knew why I had irritated you for years.

CARLOTTA
Perhaps because I loved you once, and had such high hopes for you.

HUGO
Poppycock! It was because I left you behind half a lifetime ago and your greedy female vanity has never forgiven me for it.

CARLOTTA
I was right about the brandy. You're becoming belligerent again.

HUGO
It isn't irritation that is poisoning your system but envy.

CARLOTTA
(with a sigh)
Oh dear!

HUGO
(with violence)
Envy and bitterness and regret for a life that you just might have shared if you had been bright enough to prove yourself worthy of it.

CARLOTTA
Calm down, Hugo. You'll be off the rails again in a minute.

HUGO

Would you be kind enough to get me a little water, I'm feeling
suddenly rather ill. (*He sinks into his chair*)

CARLOTTA

Get it yourself, you're as strong as an ox.
(CARLOTTA *strolls over to the window.* HUGO, *after shooting
her a baleful look, staggers up from his chair and pours himself out some water with a shaking hand. He returns to his
chair and sits down again.* CARLOTTA *comes back from the
window and stands silently looking down at him.*)

CARLOTTA

That was rude of me, I apologise. After all you are older than I
am.

HUGO

(*breathing rather heavily*)
You haven't won, you know. I don't think you ever will.

CARLOTTA

I'm not even sure I want to. I'm not even sure that there's anything to win.

HUGO

(*with decision*)
How much do you want for those letters?

CARLOTTA

I really am sorry for you, Hugo.

HUGO

That is entirely irrelevant.

CARLOTTA

It must be truly horrible to have gone through life holding your fellow creatures in such bitter contempt.

HUGO

Your present behaviour is hardly calculated to improve my outlook.

CARLOTTA

Bravo!

HUGO

Please stop prevaricating and name your price.

CARLOTTA

The letters are not for sale.

HUGO

I am beginning to think you must be a little unbalanced.

CARLOTTA

I see your point. That would explain away a lot of things, wouldn't it? Unfortunately, it isn't true.

HUGO

We seem to have reached an impasse.

CARLOTTA

Yes, we do rather, don't we? (*She helps herself to some more champagne*)
   (HUGO *opens his mouth to speak, thinks better of it, rises from his chair and walks slowly about the room for a moment or two.* CARLOTTA *sips her champagne and watches him. Her face is quite expressionless.*)

HUGO

(*meeting her eye*)

What did Perry die of?

CARLOTTA

Leukemia. He suffered no pain.

HUGO

Oh. I'm glad.

CARLOTTA

He had had a very bad attack of hepatitis the year before.

HUGO

Brought on by drink?

CARLOTTA

Yes. Yes, I think so. But he didn't drink at all during the last months of his life.

HUGO

How old was he? When he died I mean?

CARLOTTA

Late fifties, early sixties, I'm not quite sure. But he looked much older than that.

HUGO

Yes—yes—I expect he did.

CARLOTTA

He was painfully thin and he had become rather deaf. I bought him a hearing-aid.

HUGO

That was generous of you.

CARLOTTA

It was comparatively inexpensive.

HUGO

When did he die?

CARLOTTA

About two years ago.

HUGO

I see.

CARLOTTA

The only vitality he had left was in his eyes, they still retained a glimmer of hope.

HUGO

How do you expect me to react to all this, Carlotta?

CARLOTTA

Exactly as you are reacting. For the moment you are manufacturing a little retrospective regret. It may even be quite genuine, but it isn't enough and it won't last. One swallow doesn't make a summer. You didn't even know that he had died.

HUGO

How could I have known? Two years ago I was a long way away, in West Africa, as a matter of fact. I returned to Rome in the spring. Somebody told me. We were living in Rome at the time.

CARLOTTA

Yes. It was from Rome that you wrote your last three cruel letters to him.

HUGO

(*quietly*)

I want those letters back, Carlotta.

CARLOTTA

Just those three? Or the earlier ones as well?

HUGO

All of them, of course. You must see how important this is to me.

CARLOTTA

Certainly I do.

HUGO

Was it true, what you told me a while ago about this ex-Harvard professor wishing to write about me?

CARLOTTA

Justin Chandler. Yes—perfectly true.

HUGO

(*with an effort*)

I have no alternative but to throw myself on your mercy, Carlotta.

CARLOTTA

No. You haven't really, have you? I thought we should arrive at this point sooner or later.

HUGO

(*after a pause*)

Well?

CARLOTTA

If you had the choice of having the earlier letters back or the later ones, which would you choose?

HUGO

(*a little too quickly*)

The earlier ones.

CARLOTTA

Yes. I was afraid you'd say that.

HUGO

You can also, I should imagine, understand my reasons.

CARLOTTA

Yes. I understand your reasons perfectly. You would prefer to be regarded as cynical, mean, and unforgiving, rather than as a vulnerable human being capable of tenderness.

HUGO

In these particular circumstances, yes.

CARLOTTA

Why?

HUGO

Your mind appears to be so clogged with outraged sentimentality that you have failed to take into account one important factor in the situation.

CARLOTTA

What is that?

HUGO

According to the law in England homosexuality is still a penal offence.

CARLOTTA

In the light of modern psychiatry and in the opinion of all sensible and unprejudiced people that law has become archaic and nonsensical.

HUGO

Nevertheless it exists.

CARLOTTA

It won't exist much longer.

HUGO

Maybe so, but even when the actual law ceases to exist there will still be a stigma attached to "the love that dare not speak its name" in the minds of millions of people for generations to come. It takes more than a few outspoken books and plays and speeches in Parliament to uproot moral prejudice from the Anglo-Saxon mind.

CARLOTTA

Do you seriously believe that now, today, in the middle of the twentieth century, the sales of your books would diminish if the reading public discovered that you were sexually abnormal?

HUGO

My private inclinations are not the concern of my reading public. I have no urge to martyr my reputation for the sake of self-indulgent exhibitionism.

CARLOTTA

Even that might be better than vitiating your considerable talent by dishonesty.

HUGO

Dishonesty? In what way have I been dishonest?

CARLOTTA

Subtly in all your novels and stories but quite obviously in your autobiography.

HUGO

I have already explained to you that my autobiography was an objective survey of the events and experiences of my life in so far as they affected my career. It was never intended to be an uninhibited exposé of my sexual adventures.

CARLOTTA

In that case it would surely have been wiser not to have introduced the sex element into it at all. It is a brilliant and entertaining book. Your observations on life and literature in general and the people and places you've seen are witty and very often profound.

HUGO
(*with irony*)

Thank you, Carlotta. Thank you very much.

CARLOTTA

But why the constant implications of heterosexual ardour? Why those self-conscious, almost lascivious references to laughing-eyed damsels with scarlet lips and pointed breasts? And, above all, why that contemptuous betrayal of Perry Sheldon?

HUGO
(*with anger*)

I forbid you to say any more. There was no betrayal.

CARLOTTA
(*relentlessly*)

He loved you, looked after you and waited on you hand and foot.

For years he travelled the wide world with you. And yet in your book you dismiss him in a few lines as an "adequate secretary."

HUGO
(*losing his temper again*)
My relationship with Perry Sheldon is none of your God damned business.

CARLOTTA
Considering that I have in my possession a bundle of your highly compromising letters to him, that remark was plain silly.

HUGO
(*with forced calm*)
Once and for all, Carlotta, will you either sell me or give me those letters?

CARLOTTA
No. Not yet—perhaps never.

HUGO
Are you planning to continue this venomous cat-and-mouse procedure indefinitely?

CARLOTTA
No. Not indefinitely. Just until something happens.

HUGO
What in God's name do you mean by that! What *could* happen?

CARLOTTA
Unconditional surrender.

HUGO
Do you wish me to plead with you? To fall abjectly at your feet

107

and weep for mercy? Would that assuage your insatiable female vanity?

CARLOTTA

No. That would get you nowhere at all.

HUGO

What then? What do you want of me?

CARLOTTA

Oh, I don't know. A moment of truth, perhaps. A sudden dazzling flash of self-revelation. Even an act of contrition.

HUGO
(*pouring himself some more brandy*)
That, if I may say so, is pretentious twaddle.

CARLOTTA

The time has come for me to roll up some heavier ammunition.

HUGO
(*evenly*)
By all means. I find that I have got my second wind. Fire away.

CARLOTTA

Has it ever occurred to you that you were indirectly responsible for Perry's death?

HUGO

If I had murdered him with my bare hands it would still have nothing to do with you.

CARLOTTA
(*ignoring this*)
You discarded him ruthlessly, without a shred of gratitude or

compassion. Having corrupted his character, destroyed his ambition, and deprived him of hope. You wrote him off like a bad debt.

HUGO

He was a bad debt. He became an alcoholic. And alcoholics bore me.

CARLOTTA

And whose fault was it that he became an alcoholic?

HUGO

His own.

CARLOTTA

Do you really think you can shrug off the responsibility as casually as that?

HUGO

You are implying, I suppose, that my tyranny drove him to it.

CARLOTTA

Not your tyranny. Your indifference.

HUGO

Rubbish. Perry took to the bottle because he liked it and because he was a weak and feckless character.

CARLOTTA

And yet you loved him. You loved him for quite a long while. Your letters prove it.

HUGO

I should have thought that even your cheap magazine mentality would have learnt by now that it is seldom with people's characters that one falls in love.

CARLOTTA

Granted. But when the first blind rapture begins to fade, most people have the instinctive grace to accept the situation without rancour; to make adjustments, to settle for a gentler climate.

HUGO

I seem to hear the sound of violins.

CARLOTTA

If they didn't, very few human relationships based initially on physical attraction would survive.

HUGO

I must frankly confess, Carlotta, that I am beginning to find your recurrent lapses into tabloid philosophy inexpressibly tedious. You spoke just now rather grandiloquently, I thought, of "rolling up heavier ammunition." Is this it? Am I expected to stagger to my knees, bloody and defeated, under a hail of simpering platitudes? If, for some reason best known to yourself, you feel it your bounden duty to chastise me, to destroy my reputation, to batter me to the dust and to lay bare the quivering secrets of my evil soul, I have no means of preventing you. So get on with it. Attack as much as you like. But for Christ's sake don't bore me.

CARLOTTA

Like Justin Chandler you certainly are quite a smart cookie.

HUGO

I am also an old cookie and it is long past my bedtime.

CARLOTTA

Are you throwing me out again?

HUGO

Yes, I am. The "impasse" remains. I have refused to give you per-

mission to publish my letters to you in your damned book and
you have refused to sell me or give me my letters to Perry Sheldon.
There doesn't seem to be anything more to discuss.

CARLOTTA

You're bluffing.

HUGO

So are you.

CARLOTTA

I have no need to bluff. I hold the cards.

HUGO

For one thing I don't believe that this Justin Chandler exists.

CARLOTTA

He exists all right. But even if he didn't, the letters do.

HUGO

I haven't seen the proof of that.

CARLOTTA

Wait and see.

HUGO

You must forgive me if I seem obstruse, but if you have no intention of selling me the letters or giving them to me, what do you
hope to gain and why are you here? Your only explanation so far
has been that I have irritated you for years because you once loved
me and had such high hopes for me, but you surely cannot expect
me to accept that as your basic motive for suddenly intruding on
my privacy after so long a lapse of time? There must be something more, something deeper, that impelled you, out of the blue,
to launch this gratuitous attack upon my peace of mind. Is it per-

haps a long-cherished, stale revenge for some imagined wrong I did you in the past?

CARLOTTA

No. It isn't that. Although the wrong you did me in the past was not imagined.

HUGO

Through your relationship with me, you acquired a leading part which up to then nobody else had offered you, reasonably good press notices and, for the time being at any rate, an assured position in the theatre. You were praised and photographed and paid attention to for the first time in your life and you finally went off to the United States in a blaze of gratifying publicity. You cannot blame me for the fact that from then on you did not quite achieve the dazzling prospects that had been predicted for you.

CARLOTTA
(scrutinising her face in her hand-mirror)
I did well enough. I have no complaints. What I am interested in is what you got out of the deal.

HUGO
(witheringly)
In the first place I didn't regard our affair as a "deal."

CARLOTTA

Very well, I'll put it more delicately. Let's say a profitable experiment.

HUGO

In what way profitable?

CARLOTTA

That old bubble reputation again.

HUGO

What are you implying by that?

CARLOTTA

I'm not implying anything. Just recapitulating a few facts.

HUGO
(*with irritation*)
Unfortunately, I seem to have no way of stopping you.

CARLOTTA

I was twenty-two and, curiously enough, considering that I had been involved with the theatre since I was fourteen, I was a virgin.

HUGO

Are you now casting me in the role of the vile seducer?

CARLOTTA

Oh, not at all. We were both virgins. That is from the heterosexual point of view. (*She pauses*)

HUGO

Very well. I've registered that. Go on.

CARLOTTA

I didn't realise it at the time of course. You were my first love. I loved you deeply and passionately. I had your photograph on the table by my bed. I used to kiss it every night before I turned out the light. Sometimes I even went to sleep with it under my pillow.

HUGO

I hope you had the sense to take it out of its frame.

CARLOTTA

We had been together for well over a year before I began to realise my exact status in the cautious pattern of your life.

HUGO

(*turning away*)

Really, Carlotta, do you consider it entirely relevant to continue this musty, ancient, soul-searching?

CARLOTTA

Yes, I do. I most emphatically do. It was your dishonesty and lack of moral courage in those far-off days that set you on the wrong road for the rest of your life.

HUGO

It is hardly for you to decide whether the course of my life has been wrong or right.

CARLOTTA

You might have been a great writer instead of merely a successful one, and you might also have been a far happier man.

HUGO

And what bearing has all this on that dreadful wound I inflicted on your feminine vanity in the nineteen-twenties?

CARLOTTA

Because you have consistently, through all your glittering years, behaved with the same callous cruelty to everyone who has been foolish enough to put their trust in your heart.

HUGO

(*near violence again*)

In what way was I so callous and cruel to you?

CARLOTTA

You used me. You used me and betrayed me as you've always used and betrayed every human being who has ever shown you the slightest sign of true affection.

114

HUGO

In what way did I use you any more than you used me?

CARLOTTA

You waved me like a flag to prove a fallacy.

HUGO

What fallacy?

CARLOTTA

That you were normal, that your morals were orderly, that you were, in fact, a "regular guy."

HUGO

Was that so unpardonable? I was young, ambitious, and already almost a public figure. Was it so base of me to try to show to the world that I was capable of playing the game according to the rules?

CARLOTTA

It wasn't your deception of the world that I found so unpardonable, it was your betrayal of me, and all the love and respect and admiration I felt for you. If you had had the courage to trust me, to let me share your uneasy secret, not in the first year perhaps, but later on when things were becoming strained and difficult between us, if then you had told me the truth, I would very possibly have been your loyal and devoted friend until this very minute. As it was, you let me gradually, bit by bit, discover what my instincts had already half-guessed. You elbowed me out of your life vulgarly and without grace, Hugo, and I can even now remember the relief in your voice when you said good-bye and packed me off to America.

HUGO

I didn't pack you off to America. You went with an excellent contract; and in a first-class stateroom.

CARLOTTA
(*with a sigh*)
I see clearly that I am wasting my time.

HUGO
You most certainly are. And mine. The only interesting fact that
has emerged from your impassioned tirades this evening, is that in
spite of a full life, three husbands, and an excessive amount of
plastic surgery, you have managed to keep this ancient wound so
freshly bleeding. You must be suffering from a sort of emotional
haemophilia.

CARLOTTA
I salute you. You're an unregenerate old bitch!
(HILDE *comes quietly into the room. She is still wearing her
hat. There is something subtly strange in her manner. It is
not that she is actually drunk, but she undoubtedly is what is
described colloquially as a little "high." She is, of course,
aware of this and is making a gallant effort to conceal it. She
stands by the door for a moment, conscious of the oppressive
silence. She comes forward.*)

HILDE
(*tentatively*)
I do hope I haven't come back at an awkward moment. Were you
discussing anything of importance?

HUGO
No. Nothing of the least importance.

CARLOTTA
We were just reminiscing.

HILDE
How nice. It's always fun talking over old times, isn't it?

116

CARLOTTA

Enormous fun. Hugo and I have been in stitches, haven't we, Hugo?

HUGO

I wish you'd take off that hat, Hilde, it makes you look like a cab driver.

HILDE
(*with a little giggle*)
Certainly, dear. (*She does so*) I don't really care for it very much myself. (*She goes over to a mirror and adjusts her hair*)

HUGO

I see that you decided not to go to the cinema after all.

HILDE

Yes. Liesel and I just sat on after dinner, gossiping. (*to* CARLOTTA) You have never met Liesel Kessler?

CARLOTTA

No, I'm afraid I haven't.

HILDE

She is a great friend of mine. Hugo always laughs at her, but she is most intelligent.

CARLOTTA

Why does he always laugh at her?

HILDE
(*with another little giggle*)
I think because he disapproves of her. Hugo is quite old-fashioned in some ways.

HUGO
(*irritably*)

Please, Hilde.

HILDE

But it doesn't really matter. Actually she disapproves of him too.

CARLOTTA

Sacrilege.

HILDE
(*laughing*)

Forgive me, Hugo, but that is very very funny.

HUGO
(*looking at her searchingly*)

Hilde. What's the matter with you?

HILDE

Nothing. Why do you ask?

HUGO
(*sternly*)

Have you been drinking?

HILDE

Oh yes. We had a bottle of vin rosé at dinner and two stingers afterwards.

HUGO
(*angrily*)

Hilde!

CARLOTTA
(*sweetly, to* HUGO)

You seem to have a positive genius for driving those who love you to the bottle.

HILDE

Oh it wasn't Hugo's fault, not really. I just felt like it.

HUGO

You'd better ring for some black coffee.

HILDE

No thank you, Hugo. I do not want any black coffee, it would keep me awake. But now that my wicked secret has been discovered, I think I will take another little drink. (*She smiles conspiratorially at* CARLOTTA) It is as good to be hung for a sheep as for a lamb.

HUGO
(*warningly*)

Hilde!

HILDE
(*going to the drink table*)

I would have liked it to have been a stinger because they are so delicious, but we have no creme de menthe and it is too much trouble to send for any at this time of night, so I will make do with just the brandy alone.

HUGO

I absolutely forbid you to drink any more brandy, Hilde. I think you had better go to bed.

HILDE
(*pouring some out*)

"Entbehren sollst Du! Sollst entbehren! Das ist der ewige Gesang" (*She looks at them both blandly*) Das ist von Goethe. He was a great genius.

CARLOTTA
(*amused*)

What does it mean?

HILDE

"Deny yourself! You must deny yourself! That is the song that
never ends." (*She takes a swig of brandy and sighs contentedly*)
Ach das ist besser, das ist sehr gut.

HUGO
(*frigidly*)

You are perfectly aware that I do not like you to speak German
in my presence. It is a language that I detest.

HILDE

The language of Goethe is not merely German, it is universal.
You must not forget, Hugo, that my translations of your books
have earned you a great deal of money in Germany. It is ungrate-
ful of you to turn up your nose. (*to* CARLOTTA) You have no idea
of his popularity in my country, Miss Gray. *The Winding River*
went into three editions in five months.

HUGO

I cannot feel that the subject of my foreign royalties can be of the
smallest interest to Miss Gray.

CARLOTTA
(*with deceptive guile*)

Wrong again, Hugo. Everything you have ever done or written is
of absorbing interest to me.

HILDE
(*pleased*)

Now is not that the most charming thing to say?

HUGO

Miss Gray has said so many charming things this evening that I am quite confused.

HILDE

But why are you so suddenly formal, Hugo? You were calling her Carlotta when she first arrived.

CARLOTTA

I hope you will call me Carlotta too.

HILDE

But of course. With the utmost pleasure.

HUGO
(*turning away*)

Oh my God!

HILDE
(*cheerfully oblivious of undertones*)

Liesel was so amused when I told her about this strange, unexpected reunion you are having with Carlotta tonight, after so many many years.

HUGO

She must have a very warped sense of humour.

CARLOTTA

What was it about the situation that so amused her?

HILDE
(*a little giggly again*)

Oh I don't know. I expect I was a little indiscreet. But it was such a long long time ago, wasn't it? I mean it couldn't really matter speaking of it now.

HUGO

You had no right to speak of it at all. How dare you discuss my private affairs with Liesel or anybody else!

CARLOTTA

You mean that you told your friend that Hugo and I had once been lovers?

HILDE

Not in so many words . . .

CARLOTTA

Was that why she laughed?

HILDE

(*a little uneasy*)

I don't remember . . . We were just talking. She has always been most admiring of Hugo as a writer, although I must admit she doesn't care for him very much as a man. But that is largely his own fault because he has now and then been a little offish with her. We were talking in German naturally and she quoted some lines of Heinrich Heine.
"*Ich weiss nicht, was soll es bedeuten*
Dass ich so traurig bin;
Ein Marchen aus alten Zeiten,
Das kommt mir nicht aus dem Sinn."

CARLOTTA

Please translate.

HILDE

(*with a furtive look at* HUGO)

"I know not why I am so sad; I cannot get out of my head a fairy tale of olden times." That was when she laughed.

CARLOTTA

I wonder why. (*She glances at* HUGO *and laughs herself*)

HILDE

You are not angry, I hope?

CARLOTTA

Of course I'm not.

HUGO

You may not be. But I am.

HILDE

Please don't be, Hugo. You know how bad it is for you. You have been looking angry ever since I came into the room. Is there anything wrong—between you and Carlotta I mean? Has something bad happened?

HUGO

Oh no. It has all been delightful. Carlotta came here this evening either to blackmail me or reform me. I have not yet discovered which.

HILDE
(*apprehensive*)

Blackmail! What do you mean? I do not understand.

HUGO

She is a very remarkable character, a mixture of adventuress and evangelist. Her strongly developed sense of moral rectitude has impelled her to span the grey wastes of the Atlantic Ocean in order to confront me with my past misdemeanours and upbraid me for my lack of conscience. The fact that she has an ex-husband living from whom she extorts a regular income on condition that she no longer shares his hearth and home, she apparently finds in no way inconsistent with her ethical principles. All of which goes to prove what I have always contended, that the capacity of the female mind for convenient rationalization is unlimited.

CARLOTTA

And what makes you imagine that the male mind is so vastly superior?

HUGO

I don't imagine it. I know it.

HILDE

I do not understand. I do not understand at all what is happening.

HUGO
(*savagely*)

If you had spent less time guzzling down stingers with that leather-skinned old Sapphist your perceptions might be clearer.

HILDE
(*with spirit*)

You will *not* speak of Liesel like that. She is my close friend and I am devoted to her.

HUGO

Then you should have more discrimination.

HILDE

Nor will I permit you to speak to me in that tone in front of a stranger. It is in very bad taste and makes me ashamed of you.

CARLOTTA
(*enjoying herself*)

Hurray! A "sudden flood of mutiny!"

HILDE

(in full spate)

When you are ill and in discomfort, I am willing to endure your rudeness to me, but now you are no longer ill, you are perfectly well and I will stand no more of it. This very evening you accused me of being jealous of your friends and of anyone who is close to you, you even said I was jealous of Carlotta. But the truth of the matter is you have no friends, you have driven them all away with your bitter tongue, and the only one who is close to you in the world is me. And I will say one thing more. I will choose whatever friends I like and I will drink as many stingers as I like and so that there shall be no further misunderstanding between us I am at this moment going to have some more brandy. (*She goes purposefully to the drink table*)

CARLOTTA

This is certainly not your evening, Hugo.

HILDE

(having poured herself some more brandy)

Now then. I should like to know what all this is about, this talk of blackmail. What does it mean? What has been taking place?

CARLOTTA

Shall I explain, Hugo, or will you?

HUGO

No explanation is necessary. I do not wish Hilde to be involved in anything we have discussed tonight. It is none of her concern.

CARLOTTA

On the contrary, I should say that it concerned her most vitally.

HUGO

In addition to which I do not consider her to be in a fit state to do anything but go to bed.

HILDE

What nonsense. My mind is perfectly clear. Perhaps a lot clearer than it usually is. It is only my legs that are a little uncertain, therefore I shall sit down. (*She does so*)

HUGO

In that case I shall retire to bed myself.

CARLOTTA

And leave me in command of the field? I cannot feel that even for the sake of making a majestic exit you would be as foolish as that.

HILDE
(*with quiet determination*)

I am waiting.

CARLOTTA

Well, Hugo?

HUGO

Carlotta is about to publish a book of her memoirs and she asked my permission to include in it some love letters I wrote to her in the nineteen-twenties. I refused my permission.

HILDE

Why? It seems a most reasonable request. (*to* CARLOTTA) Are they nice letters?

CARLOTTA

Charming. They make up in style for what they lack in passionate intensity.

HUGO
(*loudly*)

I will explain why if you will stop interrupting and allow me to. May I go on?

HILDE
(taking a sip of brandy)

Yes dear, please do.

HUGO

I have no idea of the quality of Carlotta's book and I certainly wouldn't wish to be associated in any way with the type of sensation-mongering, journalistic claptrap which so often passes for literature in the Brave New World.

HILDE

I see no reason why you should think it would be like that at all.

CARLOTTA

Thank you, Hilde.
(HILDE *nods and smiles at her.*)

HUGO
(glaring at them both)

A little later it transpired that Carlotta has in her possession some other letters, written by me to someone else. These she threatens to hand over to an ex-Harvard professor called Justin Chandler who is apparently planning to write an analytical survey of my life and works.

HILDE
(taking another sip of brandy)

He'll do it very well. He's a very clever man and a brilliant writer.

HUGO
(thunderstruck)

What do you mean?

HILDE

Exactly what I say.

HUGO

You mean that you know him?

HILDE

Not personally, but we have corresponded quite a lot over the last three years. He wrote a monograph on you for the *Atlantic Monthly*. I didn't show it to you because I thought it might make you cross.

HUGO

Do you mean to say that you have been corresponding with this man about me behind my back, without saying a word about it?

HILDE

There is no need to look so agitated. I have said nothing indiscreet. He asked politely for certain information and I saw no harm in giving it to him.

HUGO

(*through clenched teeth*)

What sort of information?

HILDE

On dates of publication, lists of the places you have visited on your travels, a few small biographical details. He really is one of your greatest admirers. It should be an excellent book when he gets around to writing it. At the moment he is only assembling material and making notes.

HUGO

(*furiously*)

How dared you! How dared you! You have no earthly right to give out details of my private life to strangers without consulting me first. You have been guilty of the most shameful disloyalty.

HILDE

(*rising*)

I have never been guilty of disloyalty to you, Hugo. Never in my whole life. And you will please never say such a thing to me again. Nor did I give Mr. Chandler any details of your private life and you know that I would never do so in a million years. (*She turns to* CARLOTTA) These other letters, Carlotta, are they love letters?

CARLOTTA

(*extremely embarrassed*)

I think—I think I would rather not say.

HILDE

That means they are. Please tell me. It is important for me to know.

CARLOTTA

Very well. Yes—they are.

HILDE

Who are they written to?

CARLOTTA

I really cannot tell you that.

HILDE

Hugo, will you tell me?

HUGO

There would be nothing to be gained by my telling you. They were written many years ago, long before I married you.

HILDE

(*with a sigh*)

It is of no consequence. I think I can guess anyhow. But I would

have liked you to tell me yourself. As a matter of fact I would
have liked you to have told me long ago, it would have shown
me that even if you didn't love me, you at least were fond enough
of me to trust me.

HUGO

(*obviously disturbed*)

They were no concern of yours. They belonged to a part of my
life that was over and done with.

HILDE

(*with a sad little smile*)

Over and done with! Oh, Hugo! Earlier this evening, you called
me a camel, a dromedary, and an ass, but I would like to point
out to you that all those three animals are more sensible than an
ostrich.

HUGO

(*only a little bluster left*)

And pray what do you mean by that?

HILDE

For twenty years I have looked after your business affairs, dealt
with your correspondence, typed your manuscripts and shared, at
least, the outward aspects of your life. You cannot seriously imagine that in all that time you have been able to withhold many
secrets from me. The letters were written to Perry Sheldon,
weren't they?

HUGO

(*after a slight pause*)

Yes. Yes, they were.

HILDE

I thought so. As a matter of interest I found some of his replies, years ago, when we packed up the house in Chapel Street. They were in one of the pockets of that old crocodile leather briefcase you discarded when I gave you the brown one for your birthday present.

HUGO

Where are they now?

HILDE

In your strong box in the bank. I put them into a sealed envelope and wrote on the outside "Not to be opened until after my death." I signed it Hugo Latymer. (*to* CARLOTTA) I often have to forge Hugo's signature when writing his letters, you know. It really isn't very difficult.

HUGO

Why didn't you tear them up?

HILDE

Because they concerned you intimately. You are a great writer and a famous man, nothing that concerns you should be destroyed.

HUGO

Not even compromising letters that could do infinite damage to my reputation?

HILDE

It is your work that is important, not your reputation.

CARLOTTA

Think how surprising it would be for posterity to discover that you had a heart after all!

HUGO

Be quiet, Carlotta.

CARLOTTA

Actually I *have* been quiet for quite a long time.

HILDE

(*to* CARLOTTA)

And these letters you have from Hugo to Perry, you wish us to buy them from you?

CARLOTTA

No. I have already explained to Hugo that they are not for sale.

HILDE

You intend to give them to Mr. Justin Chandler?

CARLOTTA

Possibly. I have not yet decided.

HILDE

As you know Hugo's feelings in the matter, Miss Gray, that would be a malicious and unforgivable thing to do.

CARLOTTA

I notice that you no longer call me Carlotta.

HILDE

I called you Carlotta when I thought we were to be friends. But I cannot possibly be friends with anyone who sets out deliberately to hurt my husband.

CARLOTTA

You are certainly magnanimous.

HILDE

It has nothing to do with magnanimity. It is a statement of fact.

CARLOTTA

I was thinking of Hugo's treatment of you.

HILDE

As you have only seen Hugo and me together this evening for the first time in your life, you cannot know anything about his treatment of me one way or the other.

CARLOTTA

You don't find it humiliating to have been used by him for twenty years not only as an unpaid secretary, manager, and housekeeper, but as a social camouflage as well?

HUGO

(*violently*)

Once and for all, Carlotta, I forbid you to talk like that.

HILDE

There is no point in losing your temper, Hugo. We can neither of us prevent Miss Gray from saying whatever she likes.

CARLOTTA

You admitted just now that he had never said a word to you about Perry Sheldon. Has he ever, in all your years together, done you the honour of taking you into his confidence about anything that really mattered to him? Has he ever once trusted you with the secrets of his private heart?

HILDE

It was not necessary. I knew them already.

CARLOTTA

That is an evasion and you know it.

133

HILDE

You are a very forceful woman, Miss Gray, and Hugo is a complex and brilliant man, but it is beginning to dawn on me that I have a great deal more common-sense than either of you. I think I can understand why you came here tonight although I can only guess at the bitterness that must have passed between you. Your visit actually has little or nothing to do with permission to publish letters or threats or blackmail has it?

CARLOTTA

No. No it hasn't.

HILDE

Am I right in suspecting that you really came to resolve a problem of your own ego? To redress a small wrong that was done to it more than half a lifetime ago?

CARLOTTA

In a way you are right.

HILDE

I thought so.

CARLOTTA

But it is not quite so simple as that, nor as a matter of fact quite so self-centred. I genuinely wanted to prove something to him. Something that with all his brilliance and talent and eminence, he has never yet taken into account.

HILDE

What is it that he has failed to take into account?

CARLOTTA

You, being the closest to him should know better than anybody. He has never taken into account the value of kindness and the importance of compassion. He has never had the courage or the humility to face the fact that it was not whom he loved in his life that really mattered, but his own capacity for loving.

HUGO

Hark the Herald Angels Sing!

HILDE

Stop behaving like that, Hugo. You should be ashamed.

HUGO

I see that, in addition to being unpaid secretary, manager and housekeeper, you have now elected to become my dear old Nanny.

CARLOTTA

It is clear that my mission has most dismally failed.

HILDE

It could never have succeeded. You are a sentimentalist. Hugo is not. I too am a sentimentalist but then I happen to be a German and sentimentality is ingrained in the German character.

CARLOTTA

There is a wide gulf between sentiment and sentimentality.

HUGO

Turgid mysticism, Santa Claus, Christmas trees, and gas chambers.

HILDE

You see. He is quite incapable of recognizing people as individuals. His mind classifies all human beings in groups and races and types. Whenever he is angry with me he punishes me for my country's sins. He is a profound cynic which is one of the reasons he has been proclaimed as the greatest satirical writer of our time.

CARLOTTA

Why does he mean so much to you? Why are you so loyal to him?

HILDE

Because he is all I have. (*Ignoring him*) You have lived so differently from me, Miss Gray, that I quite see why you must find my attitude difficult to understand. I have only loved one man in my life, one of my own countrymen, who was destroyed by my own countrymen in 1944. When I came to Hugo as secretary I was desolate and without hope and when, a little later, he asked me to marry him, it seemed like a sudden miracle. Please do not misunderstand me. I was not in love with him and I knew that he could never be in love with me. I also knew why and was not deceived as to his reasons for asking me. I recognised his need for a "façade" and was quite content to supply it. I thought that it was a most realistic and sensible arrangement and, what is more, I think so still. I am not pretending that our married life has been twenty years of undiluted happiness. He is frequently sarcastic and disagreeable to me and I have often been unhappy and lonely. But then, so has he. The conflict within him between his natural instincts and the laws of society has been for the most of his life a perpetual problem that he has to grapple with alone.

CARLOTTA

Wouldn't it at least have eased the problem if he had trusted you enough to share it with you?

HILDE

Possibly. But it would have been out of character. He has made his career and lived his life in his own way according to the rules he has laid down for himself. Now, when the passing years have diminished the conflict, he is growing to rely on me more and to need me more, and that, with my sentimental, Teutonic mentality, is the reward that I have been waiting for.

HUGO
(*very gently*)

Hilde . . .

HILDE

Don't interrupt for a moment, Hugo, I have not quite finished. (*She turns back to* CARLOTTA) To revert to the Perry Sheldon letters. You must, of course, dispose of them as you see fit. If Mr. Justin Chandler wishes for them and you wish to give them to him, there is nothing we can do to prevent you. But I must warn you that, according to law, he will not be allowed to publish them without Hugo's written permission. He may possibly quote them and paraphrase them to a certain extent I believe, but I cannot feel that a really good writer would waste time in referring to them at all. If Perry Sheldon had been in any way significant as a human being; if he had been in any way worthy of attention on his own account, apart from the fact of his early relationship with Hugo, there might be some point in disclosing them. But he wasn't. He was a creature of little merit; foolish, conceited, dishonest, and self-indulgent.

CARLOTTA

How do you know?

HILDE

Through Liesel. Curiously enough, we were talking about him this evening. She knew him for years when she was a scriptwriter in Hollywood. She lent him money on several occasions but, as she said, it is no use lending money to the morally defeated. They only spend it on further defeat.

(CARLOTTA *gets up thoughtfully, and walks about the room for a moment or two.* HILDE *and* HUGO *watch her in silence. Finally, she comes to a halt, opens her handbag, takes from it a bundle of letters and goes over to* HUGO.)

CARLOTTA

(*holding them out to him*)

Here they are, Hugo. Here are the letters. They can be no practical use to me or to Mr. Justin Chandler. They might conceivably, however, be of service to you.

HUGO

(*taking them. His face is expressionless*)

Thank you.

CARLOTTA

I cannot say that I entirely regret this evening. It has been most interesting and almost embarrassingly revealing. If many of the things I have said have hurt you, I'm sorry. (*She gives a slight smile*) I don't apologise, I'm just sorry. I am also sorry for having kept you up so late.

HUGO

I will see that the permission you asked me for earlier in the evening is delivered to you in the morning. Good night, Carlotta.

CARLOTTA

(*looking at him, still with a quizzical smile*)

Good night, Hugo. (*She turns to* HILDE) Good night, Lady Latymer.

HILDE

Good night, Carlotta. I will see you out.

CARLOTTA

There is no necessity for that. My room is only just along the corridor.

HILDE

Nevertheless, I should like to.

(*She takes* CARLOTTA *by the arm and they go out.* HUGO *stands looking after them for a moment, then he glances at the bundle of letters in his hand and sits down in his arm-chair. He puts on his glasses, selects a letter at random from the package and begins to read it. Having read it, he takes another. As he begins to read this second one, he frowns slightly and looks up. It is apparent from his expression that he is deeply moved. He starts to read the letter again and then, with a sigh, covers his eyes with his hand.*

HILDE *comes quietly back into the room. She stands looking at him for a moment and then sits down silently on the edge of the sofa.*)

HUGO
(*after a long pause*)

I heard you come in.

HILDE
(*almost in a whisper*)

Yes. I thought you did.

HUGO *continues reading the letter as*

The curtain slowly falls.

SHADOWS OF THE EVENING

A Play in Two Scenes

SHADOWS OF THE EVENING

Cast of Characters

Linda Savignac	LILLI PALMER
Felix, a waiter	SEAN BARRETT
Anne Hilgay	IRENE WORTH
George Hilgay	NOËL COWARD

The time is the present. The action of the play passes in a private suite of the Hotel Beau Rivage, Lausanne-Ouchy, Switzerland.

Noël Coward as Hugo Latymer and Lilli Palmer as Carlotta Gray in
A Song at Twilight

Noël Coward as Hugo Latymer, Sean Barrett as Felix, and Lilli Palmer as Carlotta Gray in *A Song at Twilight*

Noël Coward as George Hilgay, Irene Worth as Anne Hilgay, and Lilli Palmer as Linda Savignac in *Shadows of the Evening*

Irene Worth as Anna-Mary Conklin, Lilli Palmer as Maud Caragnani, and Noël Coward as Verner Conklin in *Come into the Garden Maud*

SCENE I

The scene is the sitting room of a private suite in a hotel in Lausanne, Switzerland. On the right of the audience there is a door opening into a bedroom. In the centre are double doors leading to a small lobby and thence to the corridor. The furniture is conventional and what one would expect to find in an expensive European hotel. On the left of the audience there are French windows opening onto a balcony which overlooks the lake of Geneva. On the opposite side of the lake the high mountains of France stand against the sky.

The Time is the Present.

When the curtain rises, late afternoon sun is flooding through the open windows. It is a day in early summer.

LINDA SAVIGNAC *is sitting on a sofa playing "Patience" on a small table in front of her. At her right is a trolley-table upon which is a tea tray.* LINDA *is a handsome well-dressed woman in her forties. There is a knock on the double doors centre.*

FELIX, *the floor-waiter, enters. He is a very good-looking young Italian.*

FELIX

Madame rang the bell?

LINDA

Yes, Felix. You can take away the tea table now.

FELIX

Very good, madame.

145

LINDA

(as he begins to wheel the table away)
And will you bring some ice in a few minutes?

FELIX

With pleasure, madame. (*He bows and goes out with the table*)
(LINDA *goes on with her "Patience" then, after a moment,
she rests both her elbows on the table and buries her face
in her hands. She stays like this for a little and then glances
anxiously at her wristwatch. She gives a deep sigh and begins
listlessly to play again. The telephone on the desk behind
her rings. She flings down the pack of cards and goes hurriedly to answer it.*)

LINDA

(at telephone)
'Allo, 'allo—Oui—Voulez vous demander à Madame de monter
toute de suite. (*She hangs up the telephone and stands quite still
for an instant with her eyes closed. Then she nervously takes a
cigarette out of a box, lights it, and almost immediately stubs it
out in an ashtray. She wanders over to the window, stares at the
view briefly and then comes back to where she was. There is a
knock on the door.*)

LINDA

(in rather a strangled voice)
Come in.

(ANNE HILGAY *enters. She is a tall, distinguished English-
woman. Her age might be anywhere between forty-five and
fifty-five. She is dressed in a travelling suit and a light coat.
She advances into the room. She and* LINDA *stand looking at
each other unsmilingly for a moment.* ANNE *finally breaks
the silence.*)

ANNE

How are you, Linda?

146

LINDA

I'm all right, I think. (*She makes a movement towards her but*
ANNE *steps back.* LINDA *halts where she is*) It was good of you to
come—so—so promptly.

ANNE

It was a bit of a scramble getting up from the country and one
thing and another, but Gillie organized it all with her usual efficiency. I expect you remember Gillie, she was George's secretary
for years.

LINDA

Of course. I remember her quite well.

ANNE

(*after a pause*)
You don't seem to have changed a bit.

LINDA

Neither do you.

ANNE

These are the sort of things people always say when they meet
again after a long time. It's almost exactly seven years, isn't it?

LINDA

(*mechanically*)
Yes. Seven years.

ANNE

Considering that this isn't a particularly comfortable moment,
don't you think we'd better sit down?

LINDA

Of course—forgive me. (*She motions* ANNE *to a chair*) Would you
like a drink?

ANNE
(*sitting down*)

Not quite yet, thank you.

LINDA
(*her voice is strained*)

I've ordered the ice—I mean I told him to bring it in a few minutes. I didn't think you'd get here quite so soon.

ANNE

Your chauffeur is an excellent driver and, of course, the new autoroute makes a great difference. In my day we used to have to weave along by the lake. It was kind of you to send the car.

LINDA

It was the least I could do.

ANNE

Yes. In the circumstances I suppose it was.

LINDA
(*with an effort*)

I apologize for being so hysterical and incoherent on the telephone last night. I was in rather a state.

ANNE

You were certainly incoherent, however I managed to gather that something fairly serious had happened. I presume it concerns George.

LINDA

Yes. Yes it does.

ANNE

Has he had an accident?

148

LINDA

No, he hasn't had an accident.

(FELIX *knocks and enters, carrying a bucket of ice. He takes it over to the drink table.*)

FELIX

Madame requires anything else?

LINDA

No thank you, Felix, that will be all for the moment.

FELIX

Very good, madame. (*He bows and goes out*)

ANNE

(*after a pause*)

He hasn't run off with anyone else, has he?

LINDA

No, Anne. He hasn't run off with anyone else, and even if he had, you would hardly be the one I should send for to comfort me. I am not entirely devoid of taste or common sense.

ANNE

It is such a long time since I have seen you that I seem to have forgotten both your assets and your defects.

LINDA

I would be the last to complain of your perfectly natural antagonism towards me, but I think you would be wise to submerge it for the moment.

ANNE

I would prefer to decide that for myself when you have explained to me what has happened.

LINDA

Your manner makes it difficult for me to explain anything at all. You must have realized that it wasn't for my sake that I telephoned you last night and asked you to come here, it was for George's.

ANNE

Why?

LINDA

Because he is going to die.

ANNE

(after a long pause)

How do you know?

LINDA

The doctor told me last night. His name is Pasquier. He is a brilliant man. It was he who gave George the check-up last spring and advised him to have the operation.

ANNE

(sharply)

Operation! What operation?

LINDA

Didn't George tell you about it when he was in England last summer?

ANNE

No. He did not.

LINDA

It was apparently quite trivial, a small cyst under his left arm. Pasquier said that it would be a good idea to get rid of it, so

George went into the clinique for a couple of days and had it cut out. Nobody seemed to attach much importance to it. We stayed on here for about a week so that it could be dressed, then it healed up and we went to Corsica as we had planned.

ANNE

I remember. He sent me the usual routine postcards.

LINDA
(*with an edge in her voice*)
Would you rather he hadn't?

ANNE

Mind your own business.

LINDA

If I were you, I wouldn't indulge your personal bitterness now, Anne. There's very little time. You will have to make an effort to forgive me my trespasses, outwardly at least, for his sake. He will need you.

ANNE

How flattering of you to be so sure.

LINDA
(*angrily*)
Once and for all, will you stop talking like that and even feeling like that. This is a desperate emergency.

ANNE

In the circumstances, isn't it a little arrogant of you to dictate to me how I should speak or feel?

LINDA

No, it is not. In these particular circumstances there is no room for wounded pride or remembered heartbreaks or any other form

151

of self-indulgence. The situation between you and George and me has existed for seven years. I said a moment ago that you would have to make an effort to forgive me my trespasses and I added "outwardly at least." That was the operative phrase. I don't give a damn whether or not you truly forgive me or despise me or hate me or love me. You've made your gesture by coming here when I asked you to. For God's sake carry it through.

ANNE

What did this Dr. Pasquier say exactly?

LINDA

He said that there was no hope whatever. That George will die within nine months, possibly sooner.

ANNE

What is the disease? What is he to die of?

LINDA

It's something called "melanoma." He explained it to me carefully but I'm not very good at medical technicalities. It has something to do with "secondaries" occurring as a result of the cyst being removed.

ANNE

Is Dr. Pasquier infallible? Has he suggested calling in any other consultant?

LINDA

Several doctors have been consulted. George has been in the clinique for the last three days. They performed a minor exploratory operation. The findings were malignant.

ANNE
(looking down)

I see.

LINDA

That is what Pasquier came to tell me last night. He was fairly blunt and absolutely definite.

ANNE

Has George any idea of this, any suspicion?

LINDA

No—I don't think so.

ANNE

When is he coming out of the clinique?

LINDA

Tomorrow morning.

ANNE

How is he now? I mean—is he in any way ill?

LINDA

No. He feels perfectly all right. I talked to him on the telephone just before lunch. He had had an anaesthetic yesterday for the exploratory examination, but they gave him a sleeping pill last night and he said he'd slept like a log. I asked him if he wanted me to come and see him this afternoon but he said he'd rather be left alone to relax and get on with his James Bond. He was actually being considerate, I think. He knows hospitals and cliniques give me the horrors. I'm—I'm—glad he was considerate —it would have been a bit difficult after seeing Pasquier last night. I suppose I should have managed all right but I *am* feeling rather strung up and George is awfully quick at sensing people's vibrations and I—I—(*She bursts into tears. Fumbling in her bag for her handkerchief*) I'm sorry. I've been so determined *not* to do this.

(ANNE *lights a cigarette. It is apparent that her hand is trem-*

153

bling slightly. LINDA *continues to sob convulsively for a moment or two and then, with a determined effort, controls herself. She takes a compact out of her bag and dabs her face with a powder-puff.*)

LINDA

It won't occur again, I promise you.

ANNE

I'd like to see Dr. Pasquier.

LINDA

Yes. I think you should. We'll telephone him at his home number, I have it written down. He said he'd be in between seven and eight.

ANNE

What's the time now?

LINDA

(*glancing at her watch*)

Just six-thirty.

ANNE

(*returning to her chair*)

It is absolutely certain, isn't it? I mean there isn't any hope of them being wrong?

LINDA

He's a wise man, and sensible. I'm sure he wouldn't have been so—so definite if he weren't quite sure.

ANNE

Does he speak English?

LINDA

Yes, perfectly.

ANNE

Did he give any opinion as to whether George ought to be told or not?

LINDA

No. We talked about that. He said it was one of the most difficult problems that doctors have to cope with. Sometimes, apparently, mortal illness carries with it a sort of compensating illusion, a subconscious refusal to face the fact of dying. He said that in such cases it was unwise and cruel to shatter the illusion. With certain people, however, he said that not knowing was worse than knowing. Obviously it all depends on character, on individual temperament.

ANNE

I would be inclined to place George in the latter category.

LINDA

You mean you think he should be told.

ANNE

Yes. I suppose that is what I mean.

LINDA

Would you be prepared to tell him?

ANNE

Is that why you sent for me?

LINDA

(steadily)

No, Anne. That is not why I sent for you. I am perfectly capable

155

of telling him the truth alone if it is necessary. But you surely couldn't expect me to make such a decision without consulting you? You would never have forgiven me if I had.

ANNE

I should have thought that by now my forgiveness was immaterial to you one way or the other.

LINDA

You are quite right, it is. It is also irrelevant. What is relevant is that you are still his wife. I am merely his mistress.

ANNE

If I had agreed to divorce him, years ago, when both you and he wished me to, would you still have sent for me? Would you still have needed my help?

LINDA

If I considered that you still loved him enough to be of use, yes.

ANNE

Whether I love George or not has nothing whatsoever to do with you, Linda.

LINDA

On the contrary, it has everything to do with me. Your love for him, coupled with mine, is all he has to hang on to. For the next few months, all he has left of his life, he is going to need us both, and he's going to need us both on the best behaviour we are capable of. I am well aware that from the obvious, conventional point of view all the rights are on your side. You are his lawful wife and the mother of his children but if, in this intolerable situation, you attempt to trade on those rights, you will not only be cruel but stupid.

ANNE

And what rights are you intending to trade on?

LINDA

None. Beyond the fact that he is still in love with me and I with him.

ANNE

Are you quite sure that this romantic passion you feel for each other will survive the imminence of death?

LINDA

(*steadily*)

Yes. I hope it will and I think it will. However if I am proved wrong that will be my problem and I will deal with it as best I can. In the meantime you and I have got to come to some sort of an arrangement. When George is dead, when he is no longer here for either of us, we can indulge in orgies of recrimination if you wish to. You can accuse me of taking your husband away from you and breaking up your happy marriage. I can accuse you of vindictive self-righteousness in refusing to divorce him so that he could marry me. We can go through all the hoops and give vent to all the mutual bitterness that has been fermenting in us for years. But not now. Not yet. For so long as George lives, we are going to establish a truce. We are going to be friends, close, intimate, loving friends. Is that clear?

ANNE

Yes. Quite clear. But out of the question. I have no intention of pretending something that I don't feel for George's sake or anyone else's.

LINDA

I think that that sort of stubbornness indicates weakness rather than strength.

ANNE

It is a matter of supreme indifference to me what you think.

LINDA

It isn't what you or I think that counts. It is what George feels.

ANNE

You said just now that he was still in love with you and you with him. That surely should be enough to comfort him.

LINDA

That was cheap and unworthy of you. You had George's whole-hearted love for fifteen years, and even now you still have part of it.

ANNE

I really don't care for this sort of conversation, Linda. It's embarrassing.

LINDA

I don't care for it either, but we've got to come to an understanding. You still love George and you always will, otherwise you wouldn't have come here when I asked you to. I love George and I always will. In a way we're both in the same boat and in a moment as tragic and desolate as this, it would be shameful for either of us to allow our personal animosity to rock it. We have no way of knowing how he is going to react to this situation, but we do know that we are the two people he loves most. Surely you must see that if we can make him realise that we are friends again rather than enemies, it will be a little easier for him to face what he has to face. Please, Anne, give in.

ANNE
(after a long pause)
Very well. I'll give in. There really doesn't seem anything else to do.

158

LINDA

Is it a deal?

ANNE

Yes. It's a deal (*She closes her eyes miserably for a moment*)
What do we do—kiss?

LINDA

We may need to later on. At the moment I think a strong drink
would be more sensible.

ANNE

I agree.

LINDA

What would you like?

ANNE

Brandy, I think, with a lot of ice.

LINDA

Good idea. I'll have the same. (*She proceeds to pour the drinks*)

ANNE

I suppose I'm beginning to accept the truth of the matter. I don't
think I did quite, at first.

(LINDA *brings her her drink.*)

What do you think they told him—the doctors, I mean?

LINDA

(*bringing her own drink and sitting down*)

I don't know. I expect they just said that the exploratory examination had been satisfactory.

159

ANNE

He must suspect something. He has a sharp mind. He isn't the type to accept evasions without question.

LINDA

I suppose it all depends on whether he really wants to know or not. Perhaps his subconscious has already started the resistance process.

ANNE

I doubt that. Don't you?

LINDA

Yes—yes I do—but we can't tell for certain, can we?

ANNE

I must talk to that damned doctor.

LINDA

(going to the telephone)

I'll call him now.

ANNE

Shall I go to him or will he come here?

LINDA

Whichever you prefer.

ANNE

I think I'd like to see him alone anyhow.

LINDA

Of course. (at the telephone) Mademoiselle, voulez vous me donner trente-six-quarante-deux-vingt-trois . . . Merci.

ANNE

(rising and walking about the room)

I suppose he's aware of the situation, between you and George, I mean?

LINDA

Oh yes. We haven't discussed it obviously but—*(into telephone)* *'Allo. Puis je parler avec le docteur s'il vous plait? Il n'a pas encore rentrer de la clinique? Oui. Dans une demi-heure? Quand il arrive voulez vous lui demander à telephoner à Madame Savignac au Beau Rivage? Oui c'est assez urgent—merci beaucoup.* (*She hangs up*) He'll be back within half-an-hour, I've asked for him to call me here. (*coming away from the telephone*) You'd better go to him, I think. My car will take you. It isn't very far.

ANNE

(she takes a cigarette from a box and lights it)

How are we to explain to George about me being here? He'll suspect something's up the moment he sees me.

LINDA

I've thought of that. You stopped off here for a few days on your way to Italy and we ran into each other by chance in the foyer downstairs and had a sort of *"rapprochement."*

ANNE

Why should I stop off here on my way to Italy? If I wanted to go to Italy, which I don't, I should go straight there.

LINDA

You came to see Professor Boromelli.

ANNE

Who on earth is Professor Boromelli?

LINDA

He's the new miracle man here. People come from all over the
world to see him. He's a highly controversial figure. Most doctors
hate him and say he's a charlatan, but he has had a few spectacular
successes with his injections, it's a special formula of his own
apparently.

ANNE

What sort of injections?

LINDA

I don't know exactly, hormones or something—(*She tails off*)

ANNE

You mean rejuvenation?

LINDA
(*weakly*)
Yes—something of the kind.

ANNE

What nonsense. George wouldn't swallow that for an instant. He
knows perfectly well that I'd never go in for that sort of thing.

LINDA

You might have been run-down and overtired and in sudden need
of some sort of physical reassurance.

ANNE

No, Linda, it won't do, really it won't. We shall have to think of
something else.

LINDA

What? What do you suggest then?

ANNE

When in doubt, stick to the truth, or as near to the truth as possible.

LINDA

You mean tell him I telephoned you and asked you to come?

ANNE

Why not? You were naturally upset and worried about him, and on a sudden impulse you called me.

LINDA

He'd know I wouldn't do that unless it were something really serious.

ANNE

You can't fool George for long. I'm perfectly prepared to believe that in certain cases Dr. Pasquier's theory about the subconscious building a deliberate barricade against the truth is accurate, but George would never be one of those cases. He'll see through any foolish little conspiracy we cook up. You must know this as well as I do.

LINDA

Yes of course I do—but we can't be sure, can we—really sure?

ANNE

Of course we can't, therefore we can make no decisions as to whether we should tell him or not. He must take the lead. He must dictate how we are to behave.

LINDA

I'm so desperately frightened of taking a wrong step, of making a false move.

ANNE

Well, don't be. Keep your mind clear. Be vigilant.

LINDA

After you've seen Pasquier, you'll come straight back, won't you?

ANNE

Yes. I'll come straight back.

LINDA

Would you like to dine up here in the suite or shall we go out somewhere?

ANNE

I don't care one way or the other.

LINDA

I think I would rather go out if you don't mind. I'm feeling rather overstrained and there'll be less likelihood of sudden flurries of tears in a public place. There's a little restaurant perched high up in the vines between here and Vevey. The food's good and there's a lovely view across the lake.

ANNE

All right. We'll go there. (*with a wry smile*) We can talk over old times.

LINDA

(*turning away*)

Oh, Anne!

ANNE

Don't worry, I wasn't trying to dig up the hatchet again, I gave you my word that it was buried for the time being. (*She holds out her glass*) I think I'd like a freshener.

164

LINDA
(*taking it*)
A good idea. I think I would too.

ANNE
(*lighting a cigarette*)
As a matter of fact I meant it quite genuinely.

LINDA
(*at the drink table*)
Meant what quite genuinely?

ANNE
That we could talk over old times.

LINDA
Oh—Oh I see.

ANNE
The future is miserable, the immediate present appalling, so ghastly in all its implications that we can't go on discussing it indefinitely without undermining our self-control. The past will be almost a relief, even the painful parts of it.

LINDA
(*handing her her drink*)
I find it difficult to imagine anything undermining your self-control.

ANNE
I shouldn't bank on that if I were you.

LINDA
I'm sorry. It was a disagreeable thing to say.

165

ANNE

There's nothing to be sorry about. I quite see your point.

LINDA

I see that this isn't going to be very easy for either of us.

ANNE

I agree. That is why I proffered that rather withered little olive branch. You could hardly expect it to be in full bloom.

LINDA

(*with a slight smile*)

I didn't expect it at all. It took me by surprise.

ANNE

I was trying to remember that we were friends once, long ago.

LINDA

Not so very long ago.

ANNE

You made this drink extremely strong.

LINDA

Mine is the same. I thought it might uninhibit us a little.

ANNE

Are you certain that that would be an entirely good idea?

LINDA

It's worth trying. It might at least lighten the atmosphere between us a little. We can't spend the whole evening hating each other at full blast.

166

ANNE

It might on the other hand work the other way and uninhibit us
too much.

LINDA

(*holding up her glass*)

A risk worth the taking.

ANNE

(*perfunctorily raising hers*)

Have it your own way.

LINDA

Can you remember the very first time we met?

ANNE

Certainly I can. I pulled you out of the Suez Canal in 1943.

LINDA

You always boasted that you did, but it wasn't really as dramatic
as that. The brakes failed and I just slid in, lorry and all. I admit
that if you hadn't suddenly appeared with that Major What's-his-
name, I might have been sitting there now.

ANNE

His name was Edgar Hethrington.

LINDA

It couldn't have been!

ANNE

I was driving him from Suez to Cairo. It was at Ismailia that you
skidded. Actually he was rather nice, in a way.

167

LINDA

I remember he lent me a pair of slacks because mine were sodden
and made roguish jokes while I put them on behind the car.

ANNE

I can also remember the orderly's face when we dropped you off
at your base and you were trying to hold the trousers up with one
hand and return his salute with the other. (*She laughs*)

LINDA
(*also laughing*)

What happened to him—Major Edgar Hethrington?

ANNE

The poor beast got mumps three days later and everything
swelled up—they're liable to, you know, if you get it when you're
an adult—and he had to be sent home. It's called hydrosomething-
or-other, I believe.

LINDA
(*laughing helplessly*)

Cele I think—it can't be phobia because that's mad dogs, so it
must be cele.

(*At this moment* GEORGE HILGAY *comes into the room. He is
a tall man in the early fifties. He stares at* LINDA *and* ANNE
*in astonishment. For a moment they don't see him. When
they do, their laughter ceases abruptly.* LINDA *jumps up and
goes to him.* ANNE *remains seated.*)

GEORGE

Anne! What in the name of God are you doing here?

ANNE
(*rising slowly*)

Hallo, George.

168

GEORGE

Is there anything wrong with Brian or Margaret?

ANNE

No. Brian's with Andrew in Scotland and Margaret went off to Spain with the whole Chisholm family. They've rented a house near Malaga for a month. I was left alone at home so I thought I'd take a little jaunt.

GEORGE

(*looking swiftly from her to* LINDA)

Well, I'll be damned!

LINDA

Are you all right?

GEORGE

I couldn't stand that damned clinique for another minute, so I nipped out when nobody was looking, got a taxi and came home. What were you both laughing at?

LINDA

Anne pulling me out of the Suez Canal and Major Hethrington having mumps.

GEORGE

I don't know what the hell you're talking about.

ANNE

We were reminiscing—war experiences—that's when Linda and I first met, you know, during the war. We were both driving people about Egypt.

GEORGE

(*with a puzzled frown*)

I see. At least I think I see.

169

LINDA

Sit down and have a drink. You must be tired.

GEORGE

I'm not particularly tired, but I should certainly like a drink.
(*The telephone rings.* LINDA *shoots* ANNE *an agonized look
and goes to it.*)

ANNE
(*calmly*)

If it's for me, say I'm out and will call back later. It's probably
Mariette de Castries, I ran into her in the foyer when I came in.
She threatened to telephone about seven-thirty. I'll get George
his drink. (*to* GEORGE) Whisky or gin or vodka?

GEORGE
(*still puzzled*)

Whisky please, with plain water.

ANNE
(*at drink table*)

Ice?

GEORGE

No ice—thank you.

LINDA
(*at the telephone*)

'Allo—*Oui à l'appareil*—Oh good evening—how nice of you to
call—yes indeed, I did leave a message but it doesn't matter now.
Will you be at home later in the evening? Oh I see—Just one
moment while I take down the number—(*She scribbles on a
pad*) *Soixante-six-seize-cinquante-trois*. Thank you so much. Yes—
yes I'll call later on or early in the morning. (*She hangs up*)

GEORGE

That was a mysterious little conversation.

LINDA

It was poor Mr. Brevet at the American Express. I think I'm driving him mad. I keep on cancelling air tickets and then wanting them again. (*She lights a cigarette and sits down on the sofa*)

GEORGE

Well, you've got his number in case you want to cancel anything else.

LINDA

Have you seen Dr. Pasquier?

GEORGE

Yes.

LINDA

What did he say?

GEORGE
(*sipping his drink*)

Quite a lot of things.

LINDA
(*bravely*)

Did they find out what was wrong?

GEORGE

Yes. He was very uncompromising.

ANNE
(*after a slight pause*)

Don't keep us in suspense, George. It's rather nerve-wracking.

171

GEORGE

Linda asked you to come, didn't she?

ANNE

(*meeting his eye*)

Yes. She telephoned to me.

GEORGE

When?

ANNE

Last night. I caught the afternoon plane.

GEORGE

(*to* LINDA)

That was after you had talked to Pasquier?

LINDA

(*biting her lip*)

Yes.

GEORGE

(*getting up and kissing* ANNE)

It was dear of you to come, Anne. I'm very grateful—(*He leaves her and goes over to the window, patting* LINDA *reassuringly on the shoulder as he passes her. He stands with his back to them both, looking out over the lake. They watch him mutely. After a moment or two he comes back to them. He is smiling, as convincingly as he can.*)

GEORGE

What had you decided? Which of you was going to tell me?

ANNE

We hadn't decided anything. We didn't know. We were waiting for you—to—to show us what to do.

LINDA

(firmly)

What did Pasquier tell you?

GEORGE

Exactly what he told you last night. That I am going to die. Within the next nine months possibly, but probably within the next three. I will not confuse and sadden you with the details, but there will be no pain. He promised me that. He's a kindly man and I believe him.

LINDA

He told you all this just now, this afternoon?

GEORGE

I forced him to, because I had already guessed, before they did the examination, while I was waiting to have the anaesthetic I suddenly knew, with all my nerve centres, with all my instincts. It was a curious sensation, remote, detached and without fear, then. I've had a few bad moments since, but I think I'm all right now.

ANNE

You're absolutely certain that Dr. Pasquier is right, that there is no chance of wrong diagnosis?

GEORGE

Absolutely certain. Several doctors were involved. Of course Pasquier was extremely reluctant to pronounce my sentence. He was faced, poor man, with the most recurrently difficult problem that a doctor has to face, whether or not to tell the truth when a patient insistently demands it. Nine out of ten people believe sincerely that they wish to know their fate, but it is only the tenth who really means it. I finally managed to convince him that I was genuinely one of those tenth men. When he gave in and told me I was shocked beyond measure, and at the same time infinitely re-

lieved. After he'd gone I had a glass of water and smoked a cigarette and lay there staring at the white ceiling, and thought harder
than I've ever thought before. You see, I felt it was essential to arrive at a point of view to offer you, Linda—naturally I didn't know
that Anne was going to be here too—and I think I've succeeded,
temporarily at least. (*He pauses and walks about the room*) The
point of view I want to give you both is that I consider myself to be fortunate rather than misfortunate. These are not
merely brave words to comfort you with, but to comfort myself
as well. I have had a reasonably happy life, much happier and
more secure than the lives of millions of my fellow creatures. I
have done my job to the best of my ability . . . and being a publisher has kept me in touch with all the things I love most. I have
been neither a spectacular success nor a dismal failure. I have
tried to live my life with passable dignity. I have tried to be kind
rather than cruel. I have a few regrets, a few remembered follies
but I have no complaints. And now, while I have been told that
my life must end specifically in such and such a time, I have also
been guaranteed that I shall cease upon the midnight with no
pain. What more can I ask than that? Of course, I should have
liked a little longer but I have at least been allowed time to rally
my forces, and so to hell with it. That's all there is left for me to
do.

LINDA
(*choked*)

I'll be back in a minute, don't be cross with me. (*She goes swiftly
into the bedroom*)

GEORGE

Everything forgiven and forgotten?

ANNE
(*wearily*)

Forgiven at any rate.

GEORGE

I see so clearly why I married you.

ANNE

Can you see equally clearly why you left me?

GEORGE

Yes—that too. Except that I didn't actually *leave* you. I just happened to fall in love with Linda.

ANNE

It's more or less the same thing, isn't it?

GEORGE

No it isn't, and you know it. We went through it all at the time. You accepted the situation.

ANNE

I hadn't much choice, had I?

GEORGE

You could have divorced me.

ANNE

Never.

GEORGE

Why not? I've often wondered why you were so stubborn.

ANNE

The children for one thing, and my pride too.

GEORGE

Wouldn't your pride have been less humiliated if you'd got rid of me once and for all?

175

ANNE

I didn't want to get rid of you once and for all.

GEORGE

Oddly enough you won your point.

ANNE

That's good news anyhow, a trifle bleak perhaps, but better than nothing.

GEORGE

We should have had this scene before. After all we've seen each other several times over the last years . . . I've been back and forth between my two loves.

ANNE

That's a nauseating little phrase and you ought to be ashamed of such facile vulgarity.

GEORGE
(raising his glass)

I salute you.

ANNE

Keep your damned salutes to yourself.

GEORGE

This is quite like old times, isn't it?

ANNE
(suddenly heartbroken)
Oh no, it isn't. (She turns blindly away from him)

GEORGE
(gently)

I would like you to know that, in spite of all betrayals, you are still a necessary part of my life.

176

ANNE

Fine words, but curiously arid. They should have been spoken earlier. Seven years is a long time.

GEORGE

Longer than three months.

ANNE

That was cruel of you. I don't need to be reminded that you have so little time left. I am here to help, and I have no intention of confusing the issues by allowing emotion to override my common sense. I'll leave that to Linda. She's bellowing her heart out in the bedroom at this very moment.

GEORGE

I suppose I should be grateful for such stinging astringency.

ANNE

Certainly you should. It will contract your spiritual tissues and help to keep your mind clear. You have to set your house in order. There's no time to sit up in the attic opening up old trunks and sorting out dusty, nostalgic souvenirs.

GEORGE

Were you still in love with me when I upped and left you?

ANNE

What does it matter if I were or not?

GEORGE

I really should like to know.

ANNE

I see that you insist on the attic and the old trunks and the shabby disintegrated gollywogs.

177

GEORGE

Please, Anne, stop being so defensively articulate and answer my question.

ANNE

Very well. I'll set your mind at rest. The answer is No. I was not in love with you when you "upped and left me." Perhaps I was never in love with you in the way that you mean. But I cared for you deeply. There are so many different degrees of loving. How can one tell? One loves as much as one can. As you know I have never been a particularly passionate woman. I see now, in fact I've realized for a long time, that that was where I failed you. But never believe that my heart was frigid. I gave you all I was capable of giving. When you went away from me I was more unhappy than I have ever been in my life. Naturally, after a while, I got over it to a certain extent, but I missed you sadly, I still do. Perhaps I shall miss you less when you are dead.

GEORGE

Fair's fair. But try not to consign me to the limbo too soon. I know I shan't mind then but I do mind now. It makes me feel lonely.

ANNE

None of that, George, none of that. Like the reeds at Runnymede, I may bend but I will not break. So don't waste your time trying to make me.

GEORGE

Have you loved anyone else—since me?

ANNE

Do you mean, have I been to bed with anyone else?

GEORGE

If you choose to put it that way.

178

ANNE

Yes. Three times.

GEORGE

With different men, or the same one?

ANNE

Different. Three times in seven years isn't an abnormally high percentage.

GEORGE

Maybe not, but it seems oddly out of character.

ANNE

Yes. I suppose it was. But it was a sort of search really. I was trying to find out something.

GEORGE

What were you trying to find out?

ANNE

Where I had gone wrong. Why it was that I let you down.

GEORGE

You never let me down.

ANNE

(*with a faint smile*)

Of course I let you down, sexually, I mean.

GEORGE

That simply isn't true. I loved your body for many years.

ANNE

Perhaps. But it didn't love you—enough. That's why I went to bed with the others, to discover where the fault lay, with you or

179

with me. But it didn't work really. I proved nothing. I felt nothing, beyond a momentary fleeting physical excitement. I still missed you, and somehow resented you at the same time. I am sure that any psychiatrist could explain it to me in a minute, but I don't want to know, not any more. It's all too far away and the search is over.

GEORGE

I must come back home again soon. To see the house and the garden. How is it all looking?

ANNE

Flourishing. I've planted a row of tamarisks along the lower lane. They're doing very well.

GEORGE

How's old Tom?

ANNE

Old Tom's been gathered. Just as well really, he was crippled with arthritis and very feeble. Young Tom has taken over, shining with good will and more idiotic than ever.

GEORGE

When was I last there? Time goes so quickly.

ANNE

(evenly)

Nearly two years ago. You came for Brian's twenty-first birthday and we had a cocktail party on the lawn. Later we dined on the flagged terrace outside the dining-room window, just us and that awful girl friend of Margaret's.

GEORGE

. . . the one with the lisp?

ANNE

. . . Yes . . . It was a lovely warm evening.

GEORGE

(suddenly sitting down)

Oh Christ! (*He covers his face with his hands*) Fear is an ig-
noble enemy. It strikes at you suddenly, unexpectedly. (*He looks
up*) I've always rather despised people who were afraid of the
dark. Now I begin to see their point. When I was a little boy I
was outstandingly brave. I used to force myself to grope my way
about the house in the middle of the night touching familiar
things, the round silver tray in the hall where people used to leave
their visiting cards, the Chinese lacquer cabinet in the drawing
room, the china horse on the mantelpiece in my father's study, I
had to climb up onto a leather armchair to reach it. I had to prove
to myself that these things were still there, although I couldn't
see them. I wasn't commended for my bravery because one night
my hand slipped and the china horse fell into the fireplace and
broke. I was severely whacked for it the next day. But I had at
least proved that I wasn't frightened. Now it's different. There'll
be no familiar, friendly objects to touch, no china horses to break.

ANNE

Maybe the eternal darkness will be lighter than you think.

GEORGE

No, Anne. That won't wash, you know it won't, not for me. I
know you still believe, up to a point, in the things you were
brought up to believe in, but I don't—I can't. I've occasionally
paid lip service to religious superstition for the sake of appear-
ances and to spare other people's feelings, but my mind refuses to
accept hazy, undefined promises of life after death.

ANNE

There is always a chance that you may be wrong.

GEORGE

Of course there is. But I'm quite content to die believing only in life itself which seems to me to be quite enough to be going on with, and I have no complaints either except an immediate resentment that I am only to be allowed to go on with it for such a little while longer.

ANNE

If that's how you feel, hang on to it. No words can help, from me or anybody else.

GEORGE

On the other hand if, in three months' time, I suddenly find myself in some tinsel heaven or some gaudy hell, I shall come back and haunt you. But don't let go my hand—don't let go my hand.

The Lights Fade

SCENE II

An hour has elapsed since the preceding scene. It is dusk out-side and lights can be seen glimmering across the lake. There is still a slight glow behind the high mountains.

FELIX *comes in with a bottle of champagne in an ice-bucket and a tray of glasses. He puts the ice-bucket and the tray down and proceeds to tidy up the drink table.*

After a moment or two LINDA *comes out of the bedroom. She is wearing a dinner dress and carrying an evening coat over her arm and a pair of white gloves. These she puts on the window-seat. She is in perfect control and her face is calm.*

LINDA

Is it the Lanson, Felix, or the Pol-Roget?

FELIX

The Lanson, madame. Signor Luigi considered it to be the wise choice because it is a most good year.

LINDA

Thank you, Felix.

FELIX

If Madame would wish some canapés, I have them prepared.

LINDA

I'll ring if we need them.

FELIX

Va bene, signora.

183

LINDA

Has your friend recovered?

FELIX

Sí, signora. It was only a small concussion. They made three stitches in his head and sent him away, but he is most low in spirits because the police have taken from him his driving licence.

LINDA
(with a smile)

Perhaps that is not entirely a bad idea.

FELIX

But it is not quite just, madame, because it was not all his fault. The young lady in the Alfa Romeo drove across the red lights.

LINDA

Did she get concussion, too?

FELIX

No, madame, she was not hurt at all, but she was most deeply angry. It was because of her great rage that they took away his licence. She is a Swiss young lady and he is an Italian, so there was no true justice.

LINDA

True justice is a rare thing. It is foolish to expect it.

FELIX
(sadly)

E vero—La Signora a ragione. You would wish anything more, madame?

LINDA

No, that will be all for the moment, Felix. Wish your friend well from me.

FELIX

Madame is most kind—*à votre service.*

(FELIX *bows and goes out.* LINDA *looks at herself pensively in the mirror and gives her hair a reassuring pat, then she lights a cigarette.* GEORGE *comes in. He is wearing a dinner jacket and there is a red carnation in his buttonhole. He looks at* LINDA *with an appreciative smile and then goes over and kisses her.*)

GEORGE

You look wonderful.

LINDA

Thank you, darling. So do you, red carnation and all.

GEORGE

I always wear a red carnation when I'm going to gamble. I have a feeling that it brings me luck. What times does the boat leave?

LINDA

Nine o'clock. I've ordered the car for a quarter to.

GEORGE

It doesn't take more than three minutes to go from here to the Embarcadere.

LINDA

There might be a crowd. I always like to play safe.

GEORGE

Did you ring up and reserve a table?

LINDA

Of course. I also ordered a bottle of champagne. We might just as well go the whole hog. Shall we open it now or wait for Anne? She'll be here in a minute.

GEORGE
(*sitting down*)
Let's wait a while. There's no hurry.

LINDA
Poor Felix has had a trying day. His great friend, the barman at
the Hotel de la Paix, bumped into an Alfa Romeo on his motor-
bicycle and had three stitches in his head and his licence taken
away.

GEORGE
Italians shouldn't be allowed to ride motor-bicycles.

LINDA
Neither should anyone else.
(*There is a silence.*)
Do you think this is really going to work?

GEORGE
We must persevere.

LINDA
I'll do my best. I'm quite determined to. But I can't guarantee
how long it will last. I'm glad Anne is here. She'll keep me in
order.

GEORGE
We must all keep each other in order.

LINDA
She's stronger than I am.

GEORGE
In some ways perhaps, but in others she is more vulnerable.

186

LINDA

What makes you say that?

GEORGE

Possibly because I've only just realized it. As a matter of fact, I've been realizing quite a number of things during the last twenty-four hours. It's extraordinary how swiftly the mind works when faced with sudden urgency.

LINDA

We're on dangerous ground. It may open at our feet and swallow up our little charade.

GEORGE

(gently)

It's more than a little charade, Linda. Don't underrate it. The only alternative is to knuckle under, to abandon ourselves to wasteful tears and emotional chaos. And even that wouldn't last. Grief is no more durable than happiness. We should merely exhaust ourselves and each other. We can't snivel our way through the next few months just because one of us is going to die. We're all going to die eventually. There's too much spiritual defeat in the world today, too much shrill emphasis on fear. Let's stay away from that particular bandwagon. Let's, in fact, try to behave ourselves.

LINDA

Perhaps we'd better open the champagne after all.

GEORGE

(getting up)

I'll do it.

LINDA

I expect Felix has loosened the wire a bit. He's very efficient.

GEORGE

(*taking the bottle out of the bucket*)
You're quite right. He has.

LINDA

Shall we be going back to London immediately?

GEORGE

No. We'll have our two weeks in Capri, as planned. I shall have
to be back on the second of next month anyhow. There's a general directors' meeting. Also, I shall have to do some settling up. I
shall take old Fielding into my confidence. I can trust him not to
betray it. I don't want to have to face commiserating looks and
tight-lipped sympathy.

LINDA

Will part of the settling up include going back to Anne?

GEORGE

Of course. I want to see Brian and Margaret and look through
some old trunks in the attic. (*He laughs*)

LINDA

Why do you laugh?

GEORGE

It was something Anne said. She has a deep-dyed distrust of ancient souvenirs. (*He opens the champagne bottle with a loud pop*)
There. That sounds all right . . . (*He looks up at her while he is
pouring the champagne into two glasses*) Don't look so stricken.
I've been back before. Nothing is changed.

LINDA

(*vehemently*)
Everything is changed, and you know it.

GEORGE

(*handing her a glass of champagne*)

Heightened perhaps, but not changed. Here you are.

LINDA

(*taking it*)

I minded you going back before. I shall mind more than ever now.

GEORGE

Don't fuss, darling. I'm still in love with you.

LINDA

(*before she can stop herself*)

You still love Anne too?

GEORGE

(*fetching his own glass from the table*)

I've never pretended that I didn't. Have a swig of champagne.

LINDA

(*obediently doing so*)

I have a ghastly feeling that I am going to be the weak sister in our gallant little trio, the one who can't reach the top notes.

GEORGE

You are so definitely a contralto that it would be foolish to try.

LINDA

I must say something to you, now, urgently, before Anne comes back. You must bear with me. It will be a little sentimental but I promise not to go too far.

GEORGE

Fire away, fire away. I'm steeling myself.

LINDA

I know we made a pact a little while ago, the three of us, after I'd been crying and making a fool of myself. I know we all agreed that the only sensible way to behave was to go on as though there were no shadows closing in on us. I swear I'll keep my part of the bargain for so long as I am capable of it, but I must tell you now, before the performance really gets under way, that the last seven years have been the happiest of my whole life. Before we met and became lovers, I lived in a vapid, over-social vacuum. I went everywhere and I knew everybody and I never once looked clearly at myself. My marriage was a failure, my child miscarried and my divorce was sordid and humiliating. But the fact of you loving me changed everything. It gave me a new point of view and something to believe in. I want you to know that I shall be grateful to you until the end of my days. This is really a sort of spoken bread-and-butter letter and look—I'm not even crying.

GEORGE

Thank you, my love, thank you indeed. (*He hands her his glass*) You might pop a lump of ice into my drink. It's getting a bit tepid.

(LINDA *takes his glass to the drink table and puts some ice in it.* ANNE *comes in. She is wearing a dinner dress and she, too, has an evening coat over her arm.* GEORGE *rises and takes it from her.*)

You haven't forgotten your passport, have you? We have to show it when we land.

ANNE

I have it in my bag.

LINDA

Would you care for a little expensive champagne?

190

ANNE

Very much indeed.

GEORGE

(*bringing* ANNE *her champagne*)

How are we for time?

LINDA

(*glancing at her watch*)

Fine. There's no hurry.

ANNE

(*sitting down*)

I haven't been inside a casino for years. I'm quite looking forward to it. You'll have to give me some money, George. I hadn't time to get any traveller's cheques.

GEORGE

Are you going to stick to Roulette or have a bash at Chemin-de-fer?

ANNE

Roulette. I can never read the cards at Chemin-de-fer. I get too flustered. At any rate, I'm much happier just watching. I wish now I'd brought a more glamorous dress. Next to Linda I look like somebody's governess.

LINDA

I know comparatively few governesses who are dressed by Molyneux.

ANNE

It's about a hundred years old.

GEORGE

We shall be the only ones in the casino who are dressed up to the nines. It isn't a Gala night. We shall stick out like sore thumbs.

ANNE

I've always wondered why sore thumbs are supposed to stick out.

GEORGE

For the matter of that, I see no reason why we should be dressed "up to the nines" as opposed to the tens or the twenties.

ANNE

I expect there *is* a reason for it somewhere. I'm sure Mr. Fowler or Mr. Partridge would know.

GEORGE

It's curious that our two leading authorities on English idiom should both sound so ornithological.

LINDA

There's always marmalade, for instance.

ANNE

What on earth do you mean?

LINDA

I was thinking of the origins of words that have become common usage. Marmalade goes straight back to Mary Stuart.

ANNE

How?

LINDA

When she was Queen of France she was ill and took a fancy to orange preserve and everyone said *"Marie est malade!"*

ANNE

(*vaguely*)

How fascinating.

GEORGE

Do you imagine that we shall be able to keep the conversation up to this level for the whole evening?

ANNE

You mustn't be crushing, dear. We're doing our best.

LINDA

We agreed to try to behave as usual.

GEORGE

I know we did, and it was a brave resolution, but like so many brave resolutions it is liable to prove impracticable. Heroic gestures, unless they are immediately carried out in the heat of battle with all flags flying, have a nasty habit of degenerating into anticlimax. We are all three of us far too intelligent not to realize that soon, very soon, the pretence may become more of a strain than reality.

ANNE

The reality has struck at us with dreadful suddenness, George. We have had little time to prepare our defences.

GEORGE

I know, darling, I know. But even so, to attempt to silence the enemy's guns by throwing puff-balls is worse than useless. If we try to maintain an attitude of artificial casualness, the tension will become intolerable. The supply of puff-balls will soon run out and the silences between us will lengthen.

ANNE

What do you suggest? A summit conference on life and death?

GEORGE

Not necessarily, but I am definitely against a policy of evasion.

ANNE

We should be going to Geneva instead of Evian.

GEORGE

What about another nip of champagne, there's a lot left in the bottle.

ANNE

(*holding out her glass*)

Certainly.

LINDA

I'll do it. (*She fetches the bottle of champagne and refills their glasses*) Shall I ask Felix to bring another bottle?

ANNE

Oh no, please not. I'm not very good at drinking a lot. It makes me sleepy and dull and sometimes rather disagreeable, and I don't want to be any of those things tonight.

LINDA

Quite right. Tonight's going to be difficult enough anyway. Perhaps it would be wiser to go up to that little restaurant in the mountains, after all. To have decided on Evian and gambling seems to me now to be overambitious, running before we can walk. We're sure to meet someone we know and have to smile and make conversation; also we may feel claustrophobic, shut up in a hot casino waiting for the boat to bring us back.

ANNE

A quiet, romantic restaurant in the mountains would be more dangerous still. Beautiful views can be melancholy. Moonlight and stars and infinite distance are all right for young lovers, but for three middle-aged people trying to be brave they might be even more claustrophobic than a crowded casino.

LINDA

All right, Anne—I give in. It was only an idea—like the champagne.

GEORGE

I hate to insert a harsh note into this gallant conversation, but your ghastly politeness to each other is driving me mad.

LINDA

Would you rather we snarled at each other?

GEORGE

It would certainly be more convincing, and more honest.

ANNE

Don't place too much value on honesty. In certain circumstances, it can be a very overrated virtue.

GEORGE

It happens to be one of the things I'm fighting to hang on to, and I certainly can't win if I have to face you both cooing at each other like doves. For God's sake, let's chuck this bloody performance and get down to brass tacks.

ANNE

What particular brass tacks had you in mind?

GEORGE

(suddenly near breaking point)

I don't know—I don't know—and I'm not even sure that I care. All I do know is that this is wrong, deeply wrong. I can't spend the last two months of my life watching you two acting out a loving affection for each other which neither of you feel and which, considering the situation between the three of us, you could never possibly feel. I resent being treated like an imbecile and I also resent your treacly compassion. I'm going to die—I'm going to die—and, what is more, I'm going to die alone, because everybody dies alone. This fact is hard enough for me to face without your God-damned loving-kindness and pity and synthetic heroics.

LINDA
(*emotionally*)

You're not to say such things—it isn't fair. Anne and I agreed to a compromise because we considered that our feelings for you were more important than our feelings for each other. There was nothing heroic about it. We did it for your sake, because we wanted to help.

GEORGE

But it won't work! Can't you see? It could never possibly work. I know you both too well and I also love you both too well. I will not put up with tactful deceptions. The moment for me is too bitter.

ANNE
(*calmly*)

Why, George. You're positively driving us into each other's arms.

GEORGE

Excellent. A little Lesbian frolic might take the burden of emotionalism off my shoulders.

LINDA
(*near tears*)

You've certainly gone a long way away from us already.

196

GEORGE

Of course I have. It's train-fever, I expect. I'm on my way to the station.

ANNE

If that's not synthetic heroics I should like to know what is.

LINDA

I don't think I can bear any more of this, I really don't.

ANNE

You could always retire to the bedroom again in tears.

LINDA

I know I could, Anne, but however much it may disappoint you, I am not going to.

GEORGE

Things are looking up.

ANNE

What more does your obstinate masculine vanity require, George? What do you really want of us?

GEORGE

Truthfulness, a realistic view. Less tender womanly understanding and more horse sense.

LINDA

Do all men who love women despise them so utterly?

GEORGE

That is a generalization that I am not prepared to analyze at the moment. I have more important things to think about.

ANNE

Are we going to this damned casino, or aren't we?

GEORGE

Of course we are. What else is there to do?

ANNE

Well, I could go back to England, for one thing. I expect there's a night plane.

GEORGE

Do you want to?

ANNE

In one way, yes. But the decision is up to you. You're the dying Gladiator.

LINDA
(*violently*)

Anne!

GEORGE

What do you think, Linda? Would you like Anne to go back to England and leave us on our own?

LINDA

This is the first time since we've been together that I have ever known you to be really cruel.

GEORGE

That doesn't exactly answer my question.

ANNE

Your question was contemptible.

198

GEORGE

(inexorably to LINDA)

Would you like Anne to go back to England, now—tonight?

LINDA

(after a pause)

No. No, I wouldn't. I'd rather she stayed.

ANNE

What on earth made you say that?

LINDA

(meeting her eye)

Because I'm too miserable and exhausted to be able to cope with this situation by myself. Whether you go back to England tonight or not, George and I will *not* be "on our own." I don't think we shall ever be on our own again. That's all over. You will be with us if you're here or not. Therefore, you might as well stay. The charade's over and everybody has guessed the word.

GEORGE

You're wrong, Linda, you're wrong. You've neither of you guessed correctly. You think the word is "Death" but it isn't, it's "Life." If only I could make you see this there would be no necessity for any more pretence between us at all. Just now, I deliberately destroyed the pattern of behaviour we had set for ourselves because I suddenly realized how completely false it was, and that it could only lead us further and further away from facing honestly the ultimate truth that we have to face. Not only me and you and Anne, but every living human being on this God-forsaken planet. We are all united in the fear of death, we all share it, because, like eternity, it is beyond the grasp of the human mind. It is the unfathomable, the unimaginable and the unknown. But while death is the ultimate reality, it is also a negative one. Courage and honesty and humour on the other hand are positive because they be-

long to life and life, up until that last bewildering second, is all
we have and all we know. It is also our most important responsibility. The heroic figures of our world were not great because of
their strength and nobility, but because they had the imagination
to deal with their weaknesses. I happen to believe that fear is the
most insidious weakness of all, and if you two, during the next
few months, can help me to battle with that and conquer it, I
shall be grateful to you, literally, to my dying day.

ANNE

How do you suggest that we set about it?

GEORGE

By divorcing your emotions from me as much as possible and being yourselves.

ANNE

An interesting performance. I trust you will be ready to correct
us when we say the wrong lines.

GEORGE

Why are you so angry?

ANNE

Because I find the situation infuriating.

GEORGE

No longer heartbreaking?

ANNE

No—no longer heartbreaking at all . . . (*Her voice quivers, she
makes a tremendous effort to control herself, but can't quite manage it. She sinks into an armchair, buries her face in her hands,
and burst into tears*)

(LINDA *and* GEORGE *look at her in silence for a moment.*
GEORGE *goes to her.*)

GEORGE

Oh, Anne, don't, please don't. Forgive me for being so bloody selfish. I didn't mean to be unkind.

ANNE

(*in a muffled voice*)

I think I'd like a cigarette.

LINDA

Would you care for a nip of brandy, too? The champagne's all gone.

ANNE

Yes, please. I would.

(GEORGE *lights a cigarette and gives it to her.* LINDA *goes to the drink table, pours out some brandy and brings it over.*)

GEORGE

It isn't unappreciated, really it isn't. All the effort, I mean.

(ANNE *searches in her bag, produces a handkerchief and blows her nose.*)

ANNE

Good. I'm glad.

GEORGE

Do as you want to do, behave as you want to behave, I didn't mean to preach. (*with an effort at lightness*) You should never have married a publisher in the first place. You always said I was too in love with words.

ANNE

It wasn't your words that defeated me, it was a sudden feeling of hopelessness. Please don't worry. I'm perfectly all right now. Thank you for the brandy, Linda. This isn't strained politeness, it's wholehearted gratitude. (*She pauses and sips her brandy*) Are the children to be told?

GEORGE

Not yet I think; a little later on.

ANNE

And when the time comes, will you tell them or shall I?

GEORGE

You. You are closer to them than I am. They will be startled and saddened, but no more than that. I have seen little of them during the last few years.

ANNE

I think you underrate their feeling for you.

GEORGE

Brian will mind more than Margaret, which is curious really. It is usually daughters who are nearest to their fathers, but Margaret has never quite forgiven me for going away. Brian has. This is one of my deeper regrets. I love my son and I shall never see what is to become of him.

ANNE

Don't waste any time on guilt, George, what is done is done. Brian will survive, so will Margaret, so will I. We have all three become used to your absence.

LINDA

I envy you, you are better off than I am.

ANNE

Yes. I suppose I am. I have become accustomed to my own kind of loneliness, yours will be a different kind, but it won't last long.

LINDA

(*with an edge in her voice*)

Why do you say that?

ANNE

Because your temperament is more resilient than mine and your character more adventurous. It always was. Once your immediate grief is over you will begin to look about you, the world for you is still full of a number of things. You will always ask more of life than I shall. My children will eventually marry, I expect, and leave me alone and, oddly enough, the prospect doesn't depress me unduly. I shall be content to pull up a few weeds in the garden, do the *Times* crossword and look at the sea. You will make more flamboyant demands and reap more dramatic rewards, one method is as valid as the other and there is no blame attached to either. It is merely the fundamental difference in our characters.

LINDA

(*with a hint of mockery*)

Scarlet women are seldom conceded such patrician tolerance. Your manners are certainly impeccable.

ANNE

What nonsense. You are no scarlet woman, you are merely a compulsive amoureuse. Your heart still yearns for passionate love, mine only longs for peace and quiet.

GEORGE

My God! Moments of truth are clattering around us like hail!

ANNE

Which proves that our summit conference is progressing favourably.

LINDA

Later on, when we are alone, will all these wise words still be available to comfort us? Or shall we have forgotten them and find ourselves back where we started, only a few hours ago, when we first knew, when the nightmare began?

GEORGE

Don't minimize the value of words. They are our only currency, our only means of communication.

LINDA

But we can't talk indefinitely. There will be the moments before sleep and the moments just after waking, when realization comes and we shall be without hope.

GEORGE

Those moments will have to be faced, along with everything else. We can't expect to escape scot free. But the sharp impact will soon diminish, sooner than you think.

LINDA

I am sorry to be a weak sister again, but I was brought up as a Catholic and I have a sudden craving for more dogmatic, more professional consolation.

GEORGE

You mean that a priest's mumbo-jumbo would soothe you more than my graceless agnosticism?

LINDA

Not the mumbo-jumbo exactly, but the feeling behind it, the age-old wisdom, the reassurance.

GEORGE
(gently)

I wouldn't mock at your faith, my darling, or stand between you and your hopeful prayers, any more than I would query Anne's

204

sturdy Church of England rectitude. There is much age-old wisdom at the base of all religions, but for me never enough. Human beings are intrinsically cruel, it is part of their inheritance, so it is not to be wondered at that the gods they set up to worship should be equally so. Some of the old Oriental despots are perhaps a shade less bombastic than our ruthless Christian dictatorship, but they one and all smile benignly on pain and suffering and the blood of human sacrifice. Mother Nature, the Life Force, is just as bad, but at least she doesn't wrap her sadistic inconsistencies in an aura of sanctity.

ANNE

You said this afternoon that you were grateful, that your life had been fortunate. Isn't it an abuse of hospitality to speak so bitterly?

GEORGE

One may be received with the utmost politeness at Gestapo headquarters, but the politeness fails to deaden the screams of the tortured in the rooms below.

LINDA

Oh George, please don't—please don't. I can't bear it.

GEORGE

You mustn't misunderstand me. I am not denying that life can be a wonderful gift. Nor am I denying that man has achieved miracles of ingenuity, courage, and loving kindness. I am only bewailing the fact that these achievements should be so perpetually offset by insensate cruelty, greed, fear, and conceit. I am not pretending to be infallible. I do not consider that I have been singled out by some celestial agency to set the world to rights. I am merely a reasonably observant man who is about to die and who refuses to be fobbed off with mysticism and romantic fallacies.

LINDA

You can't be sure. The mysticism may suddenly become clear and the romantic fallacies true.

GEORGE

So might heaven, hell, purgatory, the bogey man, Santa Claus, and all the other nursery dreams. I make no claim to omniscience. I only know that I *don't* know and that faced with this insoluble mystery all the priests, philosophers, scientists, and witch doctors in the world are as ignorant as I am. I have no time to waste on profitless speculation, less than ever now, and I intend to utilize the days that are left by fortifying my mind against fear. Throughout the course of history, many better men than I have confronted the imminence of death with courage, humour, and equanimity and I would prefer to die, if my will is strong enough, as a member of their distinguished company. Nor will I permit myself the scared luxury of last-minute deathbed repentance. I propose to greet oblivion without apology. I wish for no cringing, subservient prayers for the salvation of my immortal soul. My immortal soul, whether it is an intricate combination of nuclei, chromosomes, and genes, or a spiritual abstraction, will have to take its chance, as my mortal body has had to take its chance for over fifty years. Every schoolboy has to face the last day of the holidays. That is how I feel now. I still have enough time to recapitulate a few past enjoyments, to revisit the cove where we had the picnic, to swim again into the cave where we found the jellyfish, to swing once more in the wooden swing and to build the last sand-castle. I still have time to eat and drink and be reasonably merry, say "Banco" at the Chemin-de-fer table, to turn up a nine and win a few coloured plaques. All I ask of you both is perhaps a little additional strength to tide me over a few inevitable moments of weakness.

(*From outside, on the lake, three hoots of a siren are heard.*)

That's the steamer. It always does that ten minutes before leaving to warn latecomers. Come, my dear ones, you have your passports. I have mine. It is still valid for quite a while.

GEORGE *helps* ANNE *on with her coat. They collect their handbags, and the three of them go out as*

The Curtain Falls

COME INTO THE GARDEN MAUD

A Light Comedy in One Act and Two Scenes

COME INTO THE GARDEN MAUD

Cast of Characters

Anna-Mary Conklin   IRENE WORTH
Felix, a waiter   SEAN BARRETT
Verner Conklin   NOËL COWARD
Maud Caragnani   LILLI PALMER

The time is the present. The action of the play passes in the course of one evening. The scene is the sitting room of a private suite at the Hotel Beau Rivage, Lausanne-Ouchy, Switzerland.

SCENE ONE

The action of the play passes in the sitting room of a private suite of a luxurious hotel in Switzerland.

On stage Left there is a door leading into the bedroom. There are double doors at the back which open into a small lobby, from which open other rooms and the corridor.

The time is about seven o'clock on an evening in Spring. The windows opening onto a balcony on stage Right, are open disclosing a view of the lake of Geneva with the mountains of France on the opposite shore.

When the curtain rises, ANNA-MARY CONKLIN *is seated at the writing desk. Standing near her is* FELIX, *a handsome floor-waiter.* ANNA-MARY CONKLIN *is an exceedingly wealthy American matron in her late forties or early fifties. At the moment she is wearing an elaborate blue peignoir, blue ostrich-feather "mules" and a hairnet through which can be discerned blue hair tortured in the grip of a number of metal curlers. Her expression is disagreeable because she happens to be talking to a member of the lower classes.*

ANNA-MARY

And another thing young man. When I ask for a bottle of Evian water bien glacée to be put by my bed every night, I *mean* a bottle of Evian water bien glacée, and not a bottle of Perrier water which is not glacée at all, and gazouze into the bargain.

FELIX

I am most sorry, madame. It shall not occur again.

213

ANNA-MARY

And you might also explain to that chambermaid, Caterina or whatever her damn name is, that for my breakfast I take prune juice, not orange juice, toast Melba and not rolls and good American coffee with cream, not that thick black French stuff served with lukewarm milk.

FELIX

Very well, madame.

ANNA-MARY

And you can tell her as well that I don't like being nattered at the first thing in the morning in a language that I can't understand. Neither Mr. Conklin nor I speak Italian and the sooner the staff of this hotel realises it, the better it will be for everybody concerned.

FELIX
(*blandly*)

Va bene, signora.

ANNA-MARY

Are you being impertinent?

FELIX

Oh no, madame. I most humbly beg your pardon. It's just a question of habitude.

ANNA-MARY

It may interest you to know that Mr. Conklin and I have stayed in most of the finest hotels in Europe and when we pay the amount we do pay for the best service, we expect to get it.

FELIX

Very good, madame.

ANNA-MARY

That will be all for the moment. You'd better bring some ice later. Mr. Conklin takes his Scotch with lots of ice and plain water.

FELIX

Madame.

ANNA-MARY

Is the water here all right?

FELIX

(*puzzled*)

I fear I do not quite understand, madame.

ANNA-MARY

The drinking water? I mean it isn't just pumped up out of that lake without being properly filtered?

FELIX

There have been no complaints as far as I know, madame.

ANNA-MARY

All right. You can go now.

FELIX

(*bowing*)

A *votre service, madame.* (*He goes*)

ANNA-MARY

(*raising the telephone*)

Hallo . . . Operator . . . *Ici,* Mrs. Conklin . . . *Oui,* Mrs. Verner Conklin, suite 354. *Voulez vous me donner le numero de Andre's, le coiffeur?* No, I don't know the number that's why I'm asking you for it . . . the place is way up in the town somewhere not far from that big bridge, I was there this afternoon. All right I'll hold on. (*There is a pause during which she scrutinizes her fingernails with an expression of distaste. She continues in her execrable French accent.*) 'Allo . . . *Je voudrai parler avec Monsieur Andre lui meme . . . oui, de la part de Mrs. Conklin* . . . pardon . . . *il est parti? Vous parlez anglais?* Oh bon . . . Well I'd like you to tell Monsieur Andre from me that the girl he gave me this afternoon has absolutely ruined my nails. I asked for Carmine fonc*ee* and what I got is tangerine fonc*ee* and they look terrible. I never noticed until I got out into the daylight. I had to take the stuff all off, and what is more she cut my cuticles, and if there's one thing I can't stand it is to have my cuticles cut, I like them pushed back gently with an orange stick and you can also explain to him that when I say I want a blue rinse I *mean* a blue rinse and not a purple dye. I've been under the shower for forty minutes trying to tone it down and—what—? Well I can't help who you are, you just give him those messages from Mrs. Conklin . . . Yes, Conklin . . . CONKLIN. Thank you. (*She slams down the receiver, rises irritably, takes a cigarette out of a box on the table and lights it. She paces up and down the room for a moment or two and then returns to the telephone, lifts the receiver and jiggles the machine impatiently.*) 'Allo, 'allo . . . Operator . . . *Donnez moi* . . . hold on a minute . . . (*She consults a pad on the desk*) *Donnez moi vingt-trois-trente-six—vingt-deux—merci.* (*A moment's pause.*) 'Allo, 'allo. *Ici, Mrs. Conklin* . . . *Je veux parler avec la comtesse s'il vous plait* . . . *Oui* . . . *Conklin* . . . (*Another pause.*) 'Allo, Mariette? Yes it's me, Anna-Mary! Why it's just wonderful to hear your voice—I can't believe we're actually here at last, I just keep pinching myself, I tried to call you this morning but your number was busy. First of all I want to thank you for those gorgeous flowers, it was just darling of you to send us such a lovely welcome—my dear they light up the whole room, they literally do—I'm looking at them at this very minute. Oh, Verner? He's all right, he's out playing golf somewhere as usual. Now listen honey about tonight—you know about the etiquette of these sort of things much better than I do—ought I to go

outside and *wait* for the Prince or will it be all right to have
him sent to the bar where we're having cocktails? Oh, he
likes things to be informal! Well all I can say is thank God for
that because I simply wouldn't know how to be anything else—I
don't have to curtsey to her too do I—I do? Whatever for? I mean
she was only a commoner after all before he married her . . . Oh
I see . . . Very well I'll do what you say, but for heaven's sakes
get here early to give me moral support . . . You're an angel!
How's dear Henri? Out playing golf too! Well I suppose it gives
them something to do. *Au revoir darling, à ce soir. (She hangs up
the telephone and heaves a sigh)*

(*At this moment* VERNER CONKLIN *comes into the room. He is
a tall, pleasant-looking man in his late fifties. There is little
remarkable about him beyond the fact that he has spent the
major portion of his life making a great deal of money. He
is carrying a bag of golf clubs which he flings down onto the
sofa.*)

ANNA-MARY
(*ominously*)

So you're back, are you?

VERNER

Yeah, sweetheart.

ANNA-MARY

You know, Verner, try as I may I just *do not* understand you.

VERNER

What's wrong?

ANNA-MARY

Well to start with it's past six o'clock and we've got to be down
in the bar and dressed by eight.

217

VERNER

What for? You said nobody was coming before eight-thirty.

ANNA-MARY

Did you remember about the cigars?

VERNER

Yes, I remembered about them.

ANNA-MARY

Well thank heaven for small mercies.

VERNER

But the store was shut.

ANNA-MARY

(*exasperated*)

Verner!

VERNER

Sorry, sweetheart.

ANNA-MARY

Why didn't you call in on the way *out* to the golf course?

VERNER

I did. That was when the store was shut.

ANNA-MARY

I only have to ask you to do the smallest thing . . .

VERNER

All the stores shut in this lousy town from twelve until three.

ANNA-MARY

Clare Pethrington told me that the Prince likes a special sort of cigar which can only be got at one particular place here, and I,

218

thinking it would be a nice gesture to have them served to him after dinner, am fool enough to ask you to take care of it for me—and what happens . . . ?

VERNER

Nothing happens. He does without 'em.

ANNA-MARY

Now look here, Verner . . .

VERNER

There's no sense in working yourself up into a state. I guess the cigars you get in this hotel are liable to be good enough for anybody, and if His Royal Highness doesn't fancy 'em he can smoke his own, can't he?

ANNA-MARY
(bitterly)
You wouldn't care if the first dinner party we give in this "lousy town" as you call it, were a dead failure, would you?

VERNER

Calm down, sweetheart—it won't be. Our parties ain't ever failures, they cost too damn much.

ANNA-MARY

You know, Verner, that's one of the silliest things I've ever heard you say. The sort of people we're entertaining tonight are interested in other things besides money.

VERNER

Like Hell they are!

ANNA-MARY

I can't think what you came on this trip at all for. You can play golf in Minneapolis.

VERNER

And on a damn sight better course too.

ANNA-MARY

You just about sicken me, Verner, you really do. Don't you get any kick at all out of travelling to new places and meeting distinguished people?

VERNER

What's so distinguished about 'em?

ANNA-MARY

Wouldn't you consider a Royal Prince distinguished?

VERNER

How do I know? I haven't met him yet.

ANNA-MARY

He just happens to be one of the most fascinating men in Europe, and one of the most sought after.

VERNER

Except in his own country which he got thrown out of.

ANNA-MARY

You make me ashamed saying things like that.

VERNER

Listen, sweetheart. How's about you just stopping bawling me out and ringing for some ice. I want a drink.

ANNA-MARY

Ring for it yourself.

VERNER

(*equably*)

Okay . . . Okay . . . (*He rings the bell*)

(*At this moment the telephone rings.*)

ANNA-MARY

(*answering it*)

Hallo . . . what . . . Who? . . . She's on her way up? Thank you.
(*She hangs up*) Oh my God!

VERNER

What's wrong?

ANNA-MARY

It's Maud—Maud Caragnani—I invited her to come and have a
drink, and it went completely out of my head.

VERNER

Well—we'll give her a drink. We can afford it.

ANNA-MARY

Here am I with so much on my mind that I'm going crazy and
all you can do is try to be funny.

VERNER

Sorry, sweetheart.

ANNA-MARY

And take those dirty old golf clubs off the couch. This is a private
sitting room, not the hotel lobby.

VERNER

I'll take 'em away when I've had my drink. She's the one we had
dinner with that night in Rome, isn't she?

ANNA-MARY

She certainly is, in that stuffy little apartment that smelled of fish. I thought I'd die. No air-conditioning and all those ghastly stairs.

VERNER

I thought it was quite a cute little place, kinda picturesque. I liked her too, as a matter of fact she was the only one we met in Rome that I did like.

ANNA-MARY

(*with an unpleasant little laugh*)

Only because she made a play for you. Why, she practically threw herself at your head, it would have been embarrassing if it hadn't been so funny. I remember catching Lulu Canfield's eye across the table and it was as much as we could do not to burst out laughing.

VERNER

Well it made a change anyway. Most of the characters we seem to pick up along the line don't even trouble to speak to me.

ANNA-MARY

You've only got yourself to blame for that, Verner. It's just that you happen to be a "taker" and not a "giver." You won't make an *effort* with people. You just sit there looking grouchy and don't say a word.

VERNER

Maybe. But I do say the five most important words of the evening. "Garçon, bring me the cheque!"

ANNA-MARY

You know something, Verner? It's just that very attitude of mind that makes Europeans despise us Americans. Can't you think of anything but dollars and cents?

VERNER

(*mildly*)

They're my dollars and cents, sweetheart, and I've spent the best part of my life pilin' 'em up, and if there didn't happen to be a Hell of a lot of 'em you can bet your sweet ass we shouldn't be sitting here worrying about special cigars for Royal Princes and giving dinner parties to people who despise us.

ANNA-MARY

I wish you wouldn't use vulgar expressions like that.

VERNER

And I'll tell you something else. This dame who's on her way up, the one that handed you and Lulu Canfield such a good laugh by "throwing herself at my head." She at least took the trouble to give *us* dinner.

ANNA-MARY

Of course she did. It was a sprat to catch a whale. Even I could see that. She hasn't got a cent to her name. She's one of those social parasites who go about living off rich people.

VERNER

Well at least she can't be lonely, the woods are full of 'em. Anyway if you think so badly of her why the Hell did you ask her round for a drink?

ANNA-MARY

After all she knows everybody, and she goes everywhere. She phoned me this morning and I had to think of something.

VERNER

She happens to be a Princess too, doesn't she? That's always a help.

223

ANNA-MARY
(*loftily*)

Only a Sicilian one. Princes in Sicily are a dime a dozen. (*She glances at herself in the mirror*) My God, I can't receive her looking like this! I must put something in my hair.

VERNER

Try a crash-helmet, sweetheart. You're sure in a fighting mood. (ANNA-MARY *shoots him a withering look and goes hurriedly into the bedroom.*

There is a knock at the door. VERNER *goes to open it.* MAUD CARAGNANI *comes into the room. She is an attractive looking woman of about forty-seven or eight. Her appearance is a trifle "baroque." She has style, but it is a style that is entirely her own. She wears no hat and a number of heavy gold bracelets. She is English born and bred and has acquired much of the jargon of what is known as "The International Set." Beneath this however, she is a woman of considerable intelligence. She greets* VERNER *by taking both his hands in hers.*)

MAUD

It's lovely to see you again, Verner. I hoped you'd be here but I wasn't sure. Anna-Mary sounded a bit "*affolée*" on the telephone this morning. I gather she's giving a dinner party this evening for our portly Prince.

VERNER

Do you know the guy?

MAUD

Oh yes, he's a horror. A great one for lavatory jokes and a bit of bottom-pinching on the side. The new wife's quite sweet and lovely to look at, she used to be a model I believe. He insists on everyone bobbing to her and when they do she's liable to giggle. You'll like her.

VERNER

Did Anna-Mary ask you tonight?

MAUD

Yes, a little half-heartedly I thought. (*She laughs*) Not that I blame her, she's probably got all the "*placements*" set. In any case I couldn't possibly have come even if I had wanted to. I'm driving back to Rome.

VERNER

It's the Hell of a long trip. Are you driving yourself?

MAUD

Oh yes. I love driving alone, particularly at night. I shall see the dawn come up over the Simplon Pass and probably get as far as Como for breakfast.

VERNER

What kind of a car?

MAUD

Rather a common little Volkswagen, you know, the type that looks as if it were sticking its tongue out, but it goes like a bird.

VERNER
(*admiringly*)

You certainly are quite a gal!
(*At this moment* FELIX *comes in with a bucket of ice. He sees* MAUD *and bows.*)

FELIX

Buona sera, Principessa.

MAUD

Buona sera, Felix. Come sta?

225

FELIX

Molto bene grazie, e lie?

MAUD

Bene come sempre. Partiro stanotte a Roma.

FELIX

Che belleza! Come la invidio.

MAUD

Evero.

FELIX

Buon viaggo Principessa e arrividerci. (*He bows and goes out*)

VERNER

What was all that about?

MAUD

Nothing much. I just told him I was going back to Rome and he said how he envied me and wished me well. He's a nice boy. We're quite old friends. I knew him first when he was at the Excelsior.

VERNER

(*at drink table*)

What shall it be? Scotch, gin, vodka? Or would you like some champagne?

MAUD

No thanks. Vodka would be lovely, with a little tonic and lots of ice.

(*While he is mixing the drinks,* ANNA-MARY *comes out of the bedroom. She is still in her "peignoir" but she has wound a blue scarf round her head. She kisses* MAUD *effusively on both cheeks.*)

ANNA-MARY

Why Maud, isn't this just *wonderful*? I'd no *idea* you were here. When you phoned this morning I couldn't believe it. I had to pinch myself. My! But you look cute as a June bug with all those gorgeous bangles. Come and sit down right here and tell me all the gossip. How's dear Lulu?

MAUD

(*sitting*)

I don't know. I haven't seen her for ages. I've been here for the last two weeks staying with my son and his wife.

ANNA-MARY

Why, Maud! You take the breath right out of my body! Nobody ever told me you had a son!

MAUD

It isn't exactly a topic of universal interest.

ANNA-MARY

But how old is he? What does he *do*? Is he handsome? Do you adore him? I've just got to meet him.

MAUD

I don't think he's really your cup of tea. He paints abstract pictures and he's a Communist.

ANNA-MARY

(*shocked to the marrow*)

A Communist!

MAUD

I don't mean that he's actually a member of the "party" but he's terribly red-minded. He's also going through a grubby phase at the moment. They have a ghastly little flat in Pully and a lot of Beatnik cronies. It's all quite fun really.

227

VERNER

(handing her a vodka and tonic)

Here's your booze, Princess.

MAUD

(taking it)

Thanks pal.

ANNA-MARY

And you say he's got a wife?

MAUD

Yes, she's small and sharp, like a little needle. She used to be a dancer in the Festival ballet and she's just had a baby. That's why I've been here for so long, it sort of hung back. All those *Giselles* and *Swan Lakes* make child-bearing a little complicated.

ANNA-MARY

And she had the baby? *(Offering a cigarette)*

MAUD

Yes. No, thank you. *(Refuses it)* Late last night, in the hospital. It's a boy and it weighed exactly what it ought to weigh and was bright red, possibly out of deference to its father's political views. Anyhow I am now a grandmother which is a sobering thought.

ANNA-MARY

No one would believe it. You look sensational!

MAUD

(sipping her drink)

So do you, Anna-Mary, so do you. That particular colour is very becoming.

ANNA-MARY

Yes, nice, isn't it?

228

MAUD

Now I come to think of it you wore blue that night in Rome when you came to dine.

ANNA-MARY

And how is that *divine* little apartment? I was saying to Clare Pethrington at lunch today that it was just *the* most picturesque place I ever saw, wasn't I, Verner?

VERNER
(*laconically*)

Yes, sweetheart.

MAUD

Clare hates it. She says there are too many stairs and that it smells of fish. Which is only to be expected really because there happens to be a fishmonger on the ground floor. I keep on burning incense and dabbing the light bulbs with "Miss Dior" but it doesn't do any good.

ANNA-MARY

You know I'm just heart-broken that you can't come to dinner tonight. It's going to be loads of fun. I've got Mariette and Henri, the Pethringtons of course, Sir Gerard and Lady Nutfield, he was the Governor of somewhere or other and he looks so British you just want to stand up and sing "God Save the Queen" the moment he comes into the room! Then there are the Carpinchos, they're Brazilian and as cute as they can be, and Bobo Larkin who's promised to play the piano in the bar afterwards providing we keep everybody out, and darling old Irma Bidmeyer who lives in this very hotel and plays Bridge with the Queen of Spain, and, last but not least, Their Royal Highnesses!

MAUD

Not Royal, dear, just Serene.

229

ANNA-MARY

(*visibly shaken*)

Maud! Is that really true? Are you positive?

MAUD

Quite. But you needn't worry about it, it doesn't make any difference. So long as everybody calls him "Sir" and bobs up and down like a cork, he's as happy as a clam.

ANNA-MARY

But I could have *sworn* that Mariette said . . .

MAUD

(*laughing*)

Mariette's terribly vague about that sort of thing. She once lost her head at an official reception in Geneva and addressed poor old Prince Paniowtovski as "Ma'am!" She wasn't far out at that.

VERNER

(*with a guffaw*)

You know that's funny! That's very funny!

ANNA-MARY

(*ignoring this*)

Do you mean I have to *introduce* him as His Serene Highness?

MAUD

You don't have to introduce him at all. You just take people up to him and say: "Sir—may I present so-and-so." He may buck a bit at Irma Bidmeyer, he's notoriously anti-Semitic, but you can always mumble.

VERNER

Well—what do you know?

ANNA-MARY
(*crossly*)

Do be quiet, Verner, and stop interrupting.

VERNER

Okay, sweetheart.

ANNA-MARY

Why don't you make yourself useful for once and go down to the bar and ask if they've got any of those cigars. I want to have a little private visit with Maud.

VERNER

Okay, sweetheart.

ANNA-MARY

And for heaven's sakes take those golf clubs with you.

MAUD

Oh, don't send him away. I've hardly talked to him at all.

VERNER

Don't worry, Princess. I'll just set the table, fix the flowers, give a hundred dollars to each of the waiters and be right back. (*He winks at her, picks up his golf bag and goes out.*)
(ANNA-MARY *sighs heavily.*)

ANNA-MARY

Verner really gets on my nerves sometimes.

MAUD
(*quizzically*)

Yes. I see he does.

ANNA-MARY

He's just plain stubborn. He refuses to be interested in any of the things I'm interested in, he doesn't like any of the people I like.

MAUD

He doesn't seem to mind me.

ANNA-MARY

Only because you lay yourself out to be nice to him.

MAUD

Perhaps that's what he needs.

ANNA-MARY

You were just darling to him that night we dined with you. I remember saying to Lulu afterwards, Maud's just wonderful, she's warm, she's human, and what's more, she's a giver and not a taker.

MAUD

You mustn't overrate me, Anna-Mary. I'm a taker all right when I get the chance.

ANNA-MARY

Why, Maud Caragnani, that's just plain nonsense and you know it! You can't fool me. The one thing I flatter myself I'm never wrong about is people. Why do you suppose it is that you're so popular? That everybody's always running after you and asking you everywhere?

MAUD

It's very sweet of you to say so, but I'm afraid you exaggerate my social graces.

ANNA-MARY

I'm not talking about social graces honey. I'm talking about "character" and "heart"! You're just basically *"sympathique"* and there's no getting away from it! And above all you go through life *making an effort!* Now Verner just will not make an effort. He just stands around waiting for people to come to him, instead of him going to them. Do you see what I mean?

MAUD

Perfectly. But I find it difficult to believe that he could have made the enormous fortune he has, if he were all that lackadaisical.

ANNA-MARY

Oh he's sharp enough in business, I'll grant you that, but he just won't open his arms out to *experience.* I mean he deliberately shuts his eyes to the *beauty* of things. You'd never credit it but in the whole five months we've been in Europe this trip, he's only been inside three churches!

MAUD
(*laughing*)
Perhaps he doesn't like churches.

ANNA-MARY

I managed to drag him into Saint Peter's in Rome and all he did was stomp around humming "I Like New York in June" under his breath. I was mortified.

MAUD

Oh poor Buffalo Bill!

ANNA-MARY

What on *earth* do you mean by that?

MAUD

It's how I see Verner in my mind's eye. A sort of frustrated Buffalo Bill who's had his horse taken away from him.

ANNA-MARY
(snappily)

Verner can't ride horseback.

MAUD

There's still time for him to learn.

ANNA-MARY

He's turned fifty-five. His arteries wouldn't stand it.

MAUD

There are different sorts of horses. Pegasus, for instance. He had wings.

ANNA-MARY

You know something, Maud? I just haven't the faintest idea what you're talking about.

MAUD

Verner. We're both talking about Verner. But from different points of view.

(*The telephone rings.* ANNA-MARY, *with an exclamation of irritation, gets up and goes over to it.*)

ANNA-MARY
(*lifting the receiver*)

Hallo . . . Yes, speaking . . . Bobo! My dear . . . I never recognized your voice. What! You can't mean it . . . you can't be serious! But when did it happen . . . I mean you sounded perfectly all right on the phone this morning . . . Oh my God! (*There is an anguished pause while she listens.*) But Bobo you

234

can't do this to me, at the very last minute. I just can't stand it
. . . But if you don't come we shall be thirteen at table . . . But
Bobo honey, I was *counting* on you! I've made all the arrangements about the piano in the bar after dinner and everything . . .
Well all I can say is that it's just disaster that's all, absolute disaster . . . Couldn't you just manage to come for dinner? That
would be better than nothing . . . A hundred and two! Are you
sure it's a hundred and two? When did you take it? What—the
doctor says you're not to talk any more on the phone—but Bobo
—Bobo—(*She closes her eyes in despair and hangs up the receiver*) He hung up on me. He just hung up on me! After dealing
me the worst blow in my life he has the nerve to hang up on me.
I'll never speak to that God damned little pansy again as long as
there's breath left in my body.

MAUD

Be reasonable, Anna-Mary. You can't expect the poor beast to
come to dinner if he's got a temperature of a hundred and two.

ANNA-MARY

Reasonable! Seven o'clock, thirteen at table, and you ask me to
be reasonable!

MAUD

Can you think of anyone else?

ANNA-MARY

Of course I can't. We only got here last night. You'll have to
come, Maud, you'll just *have* to. It'll make one woman too many
but that can't be helped.

MAUD

I really can't possibly. I haven't even got an evening dress with
me, and I have to drive to Rome.

ANNA-MARY

Oh Maud, go to Rome later, go to Rome any time but just help me out tonight. You don't have to worry about an evening dress. I can lend you a divine Balenciaga model I've only worn twice. Oh Maud, for heaven's sakes I don't know where I'm at. This is a ghastly situation. I think I'm going crazy.

MAUD

Why don't you call up Mariette? She might have somebody on tap for just this sort of crisis.

ANNA-MARY

You really won't come? I'd bless you until my dying day if only you would.

MAUD
(*shaking her head*)
It's quite out of the question.

ANNA-MARY

You mean you don't *want* to come.

MAUD

To be perfectly frank I don't. In the first place I haven't spoken to either of the Pethringtons for three years, I can't stand the sight of dear old Irma Bidmeyer and I think the Prince is the most lascivious, vulgar old bore it has ever been my misfortune to meet.

ANNA-MARY
(*outraged at such lèse-majesté*)
Maud!

MAUD

But leaving all that aside I've promised to pick up my son at the hospital and take him to dine at the Grappe d'Or. They probably won't let him in if he looks anything like he looked earlier in the day, but it's the last chance I shall have of seeing him for a long time. Why don't you call up Mariette as I suggested?

ANNA-MARY
(*going to the telephone*)
This is ghastly—just ghastly!

MAUD
Don't take it so hard Anna-Mary. I'm quite sure the Prince would waive the most atavistic superstition for the sake of a free meal.

ANNA-MARY
I just don't know how you can sit there Maud and say such terrible things.

MAUD
We just happen to be talking about the same person from different points of view again don't we? Only in this case I happen to know him and you don't.

ANNA-MARY
(*at the telephone*)
Operator . . . Operator . . . *Donnez moi* . . . (*She glances at the pad again*) *Donnez moi vingt-trois-trente-six-vingt-deux s'il vous plait et aussi vite que possible on account of je suis pressé.* (*Balefully to* MAUD) The next time I see that Bobo Larkin, I'll just make him wish he'd never been born.

MAUD
He's probably wishing that at this very moment if he's got a temperature of a hundred and two.

ANNA-MARY
(*at the telephone again*)
'Allo . . . 'Allo . . . *Ici*, Mrs. Conklin, *je veux parler avec la com-*

237

tesse s'il vous plait . . . what? I mean *comment? (She listens for a moment or two) Je ne comprends pas—parlez vous Anglais.* (*to* MAUD) It's a different man from the one I talked to before. I can't understand a word he's saying . . .

MAUD
(*rising*)

Give it to me. (*She takes the telephone*) 'Allo . . . *C'est de la part de Madame Conklin, est ce que Madame la comtesse est la? Oui . . . Elle est sortie? Depuis quand? Vous savez ou? Oui j'ecoute, un cocktail chez Madame de Vosanges . . . Oui . . . vous ne savez pas le numero par hazard . . . Ah bon, je vais le chercher . . . Merci beaucoup.* (*She hangs up*) She left ten minutes ago to go to a cocktail party and she's not coming back before dinner.

ANNA-MARY
I think I'm going out of my mind!

MAUD
Somebody called Vosanges. I don't know them, but they're sure to be in the book. (*She starts to look in the telephone book when* VERNER *comes into the room.*)

VERNER
What's cooking?

ANNA-MARY
The most terrible thing's happened.

MAUD
(*looking up from the telephone book*)
Bobo Larkin's got a temperature of a hundred and two.

VERNER
Well—what do you know? Who the Hell's Bobo Larkin?

ANNA-MARY
(*with dreadful patience*)

It doesn't matter *who* he is, Verner. But what does matter is *where* he is. And *where* he is is in bed with a fever which means that he can't come to dinner, nor can he play the piano in the bar *after* dinner.

VERNER

Poor guy. Probably a virus of some sort.

ANNA-MARY

It can be a virus or bubonic plague for all I care, but what it means is that we shall be thirteen at table.

VERNER

Well—well—well! Boy, are we in trouble? (*He laughs*)

ANNA-MARY
(*icily*)

There's nothing to laugh about, Verner. It'll *ruin* the whole evening.

VERNER

Sorry, sweetheart. It's just nerves. (*to* MAUD) What about you, Princess? How about you pinch-hitting for this Bozo what's his name?

MAUD

Not even for you, Verner. Also I can't play the piano, in the bar or anywhere else. I've found the number, Anna-Mary. Do you want me to ring it and see if I can get hold of Mariette?

ANNA-MARY

No, it's too late. And anyway I couldn't have her just dragging *anyone* along to meet Royalty. There's only one thing to be done. Verner, you must have your dinner up here.

239

VERNER

Huh?

MAUD

Won't that seem a little odd?

ANNA-MARY

It can't be helped. We'll pretend you're sick or something.

VERNER

You can say I've got a temperature of a hundred and three!

ANNA-MARY

You *could* be waiting for an important business call from New York.

MAUD

No, Anna-Mary. I don't think that would do. A high fever would be more convincing. You can't fob off a Serene Highness with a mere business call. It would be *lèse-majesté*.

VERNER

You could always say I've got a galloping hernia.

ANNA-MARY

(losing her temper)

You think this is very funny, don't you? Both you and Maud? Well, all I can say is I'm very very sorry I can't share the joke. Mariette's been just wonderful making arrangements for this dinner for me tonight. We've been phoning each other back and forth for weeks. She's the only one who has taken the trouble to plan it all for *my* sake, and if only for *her* sake I'm going to see that it's a success if it's the last thing I do. And I'd like to say one thing more because I just can't keep it in any longer. I'm bitterly disappointed in you, Maud, and it's no use pretending I'm not. I

240

think it's real mean of you not to stand by me tonight and help me out of this jam. You could perfectly easily come to dinner if you wanted to.

MAUD

(*calmly*)

Certainly I could but, as I have already explained to you, I don't want to, and, as you may remember, I also explained why.

ANNA-MARY

I can remember that you were insulting about my guests and said the Prince was vulgar, and I just don't happen to think that's a nice way to talk.

VERNER

Listen sweetheart, let's not have a brawl, shall we?

ANNA-MARY

(*ignoring him, to* MAUD)

You've hurt me, Maud, more than I can say. You've let me down. And I thought you were a friend.

MAUD

(*coldly*)

Why?

VERNER

Holy mackerel!

MAUD

(*inexorably to* ANNA-MARY)

We have met casually three or four times and you have dined with me once. Is that, according to your curious code of behaviour, sufficient basis for a life-long affection?

241

ANNA-MARY

(*with grandeur*)

I do not give my friendship as easily as you seem to think, Maud, and when I do it is only to those who are truly sincere and willing to stand by me in time of trouble. After all that is what friendship is for, isn't it? It's a question of give and take. However I do not wish to discuss the matter any further. I am sorry that there should have been this little misunderstanding between us, and I can only hope that the next time our paths cross, the clouds will have rolled away and everything will be forgiven and forgotten. If you will excuse me now I must go and dress and do my hair. Verner, you will have your dinner up here, and can ring for the waiter and order it whenever you feel like it. And I'd be very glad if you would ring down to the Maitre D and tell him I'll be in the dining room at eight o'clock to rearrange the place cards. (*She bows coldly to* MAUD *and goes into the bedroom*)

MAUD

(*after a pause*)

Well that's that, isn't it?

VERNER

She sure is good and mad.

MAUD

Oh I'm sorry. I'm afraid it's partly my fault. I was rather beastly to her.

VERNER

Forget it. Anna-Mary's tough, she can take it.

MAUD

Yes, I'm sure she can. But I hate being beastly to people. It's only that she made me suddenly angry. I wish I hadn't been.

VERNER

Have another drink.

MAUD

No thank you. I really must go now.

VERNER

Come on, just a small one.

MAUD

(*glancing at her watch*)

Very well, but make it a really small one. I must leave at a quarter past.

VERNER

(*going to the drink table*)

Atta girl!

MAUD

(*sitting down*)

What an idiotic little drama. (*She sighs*) Oh dear!

VERNER

Snap out of it, Princess. It ain't worth worrying about. Anna-Mary always raises Hell when things don't happen to go just the way she wants.

MAUD

Yes. I expect she does.

VERNER

I don't pay no mind to it any more.

MAUD

Are you disappointed? About being forbidden to go to your own dinner party I mean?

VERNER

It's just about breaking my heart.

MAUD

(*with a smile*)

Yes. I suspect it is. (*She raises her glass to him*) Well, here's to the next time we meet. When all those clouds have rolled away and everything is forgiven and forgotten.

VERNER

(*raising his glass*)

Here's to the next time we meet anyway, whether everything's been forgiven and forgotten or not.

MAUD

Thank you, Verner. I'll remember that.

VERNER

Do you want to know something?

MAUD

Shoot pal.

VERNER

That evening we had with you in Rome was the highspot of our whole trip—for me.

MAUD

Only because I "laid myself out to be nice to you." That's what Anna-Mary told me earlier on this evening.

VERNER

Well, Momma was dead on the nose for once. You sure did.

MAUD

And it worked apparently.

244

VERNER

Princess, it worked like a charm.

MAUD

Would you mind if I asked you a very personal question, almost an impertinent one as a matter of fact?

VERNER

Go right ahead.

MAUD

You really are a very very rich man, aren't you?

VERNER

If that's the question, I guess the answer's yes.

MAUD

It isn't. The question is more complicated than that, and I wouldn't even ask it if I didn't like you enough to be genuinely interested. (*She pauses*)

VERNER

(*sipping his drink and looking at her*)

Well?

MAUD

Why, when you can easily afford to do whatever you like, do you allow yourself to be continually bullied into doing what you don't like?

VERNER

That sure is a sixty-four thousand dollar question all right.

MAUD

You must have asked it to yourself occasionally. You're nobody's fool.

245

VERNER
(*looking down*)
Maybe I have, Princess. Maybe I have.

MAUD
And did you give yourself the sixty-four thousand dollar answer?

VERNER
(*looking down*)
No, Princess. I guess I goofed it.

MAUD
Yes, dear Buffalo Bill. I'm sadly afraid you did.

VERNER
Hey! What's this Buffalo Bill bit?

MAUD
Just one of my little personal fantasies. I puzzled Anna-Mary with it a short while ago. I said you needed a horse.

VERNER
A horse! Are you out of your mind? What the Hell should I do with a horse?

MAUD
(*laughing*)
Jump on its back and gallop away on it. Failing a horse, a dolphin would be better than nothing. There was a little boy in Greek mythology I believe who had an excellent seat on a dolphin. It took him skimming along over the blue waves of the Aegean, and he never had to go to any dinner parties or meet any important people and whenever they came to rest on a rock or a little white beach, the dolphin would dive deep deep down and bring him up a golden fish. It's high time somebody gave you a golden fish,

246

Verner. It would mean nothing on the Stock Exchange but it might light up your whole sad world.

VERNER
(*astonished*)

Well I'll be God damned!

MAUD
(*rising purposefully*)

I must go now. I promised my son I'd be at the hospital at seven-thirty.

VERNER
(*with feeling*)

Don't go yet, Princess. Please don't go yet.

MAUD

I can't. I really can't. But we'll meet again. (*She unexpectedly kisses him on the cheek*) Good-bye for the moment, dear Buffalo Bill. Don't forget me too soon.

She goes swiftly out of the room as

The lights fade

SCENE TWO

Several hours have passed and it is now about eleven o'clock in the evening.

When the lights fade in on the scene, VERNER *is stretched out on the sofa reading an Ian Fleming novel. He has taken off his tie and his shirt is open at the neck. On stage Right there is a table with the remains of his dinner on it.*

There is a discreet knock on the door.

VERNER

Come in. *Entrez.*
(FELIX *comes in bearing a bottle of Evian water in a large bucket of ice.*)

FELIX

I hope I do not intrude, monsieur, but Madame requested a bottle of Evian bien glacée to be put by her bed.

VERNER

Okay. Go right ahead.
(FELIX *takes the Evian into the bedroom. After a moment he reappears.*)

FELIX

I regret not having taken away the table before, monsieur, but I am singlehanded on this floor tonight and there has been much to do.

VERNER

Don't worry, that's all right with me.

248

FELIX

Monsieur has need of anything?

VERNER

(*thoughtfully*)

Yeah, it seems that I have. I have need of a golden fish.

FELIX

Pardon, monsieur?

VERNER

Never mind. Skip it. Give me a bourbon on the rocks.

FELIX

Bien, monsieur. (*He goes to the drink table*)

VERNER

Princess Caragnani said she knew you before. In Rome, wasn't it?

FELIX

Yes sir. I served in the bar at the Excelsior for several months. Only as third barman though. The Princess often was there with friends.

VERNER

She has a lot of friends in Rome, hasn't she?

FELIX

(*with enthusiasm*)

Ah si signore, e una donna molto incantevole, tutto il mondo . . .

VERNER

Hey, none of that, stick to English.

FELIX

I was saying that she is a lady much enchanted and that all the world are most fond of her.

VERNER

(*a little wistfully*)

Yeah, I'll bet they are.

FELIX

(*handing him his drink*)

Your drink, monsieur.

VERNER

Thanks. (*He takes it*) Molto gratzie!

FELIX

(*delighted*)

Ah Bravo! *Il signore cominca imparare l'Italiano!* Monsieur is beginning to learn my language.

VERNER

I guess it's never too late to try—to try to learn someone else's language.

FELIX

It is difficult at first, but here in La Suisse there is much opportunity because there are so many languages spoken.

VERNER

(*with a little laugh*)

You're telling me! Have you got a girl?

FELIX

Oh yes, monsieur.

VERNER

Is she here in Lausanne?

FELIX

No, signore. She is in Italy.

VERNER

What's her name?

FELIX

Renata.

VERNER

Are you crazy about her?

FELIX

No, signore. But we are most fond. I have taught her to water-ski.

VERNER

Are you going to marry her?

FELIX

(*with a slight shrug*)

Che sa? One day perhaps, but first I must make the money to afford it.

VERNER

Can you ride horseback?

FELIX

(*puzzled*)

No, signore. But in the village where I was born my Uncle had a mule which I used to ride in the mountains. *Era un animale molto cattivo.* It was a most angry animal.

251

VERNER

And a dolphin, did you ever try a dolphin, when you were a kid?

FELIX

I fear I do not understand.

VERNER

You know, a porpoise—a kinda fish—(*He makes a gesture illustrating a porpoise jumping*)
>   (FELIX *looks at him in some dismay.*)

FELIX

Ah si—un porco marino—un delfino! Monsieur makes the little joke?

VERNER

Yeah. I guess you're right. It was only a little joke.

FELIX

Is there anything more that Monsieur requires?

VERNER

Yeah Felix. I'm beginning to think there is. You can take away the table now.

FELIX

Bien, monsieur.
>   (VERNER *takes a roll of bills from his pocket and gives one to* FELIX.)

VERNER

Here. Buy a present for Renata.

FELIX

(*looking at it*)
Monsieur has made a mistake. This is fifty dollars.

252

VERNER

No, Felix. It ain't no mistake. I guess the only thing that Monsieur never makes a mistake about is money. Have yourself a ball. Good night Felix.

FELIX

(*overwhelmed*)

Mille mille grazie, signore . . . Monsieur is most generous. *A domani, signore, a domani.*

(FELIX *bows and wheels the dinner table from the room.* VERNER, *left alone, returns to his book, tries to read it for a moment or two and then flings it down. He is about to light a cigarette when the telephone rings. He goes to it.*)

VERNER

(*at the telephone*)

Hallo . . . Yes, speaking (*His voice lightens*) Oh it's you! Where are you? Here in the lobby? Yeah . . . come on up . . . come right on up.

(VERNER *replaces the receiver and sits staring at the telephone for a second with a beaming smile. He then jumps to his feet, runs to the mirror, smooths his hair and straightens his tie. Then he hurriedly puts on his shoes and his coat, goes back again to the mirror to reassure himself, gulps down the remainder of his bourbon and lights, with a slightly trembling hand, the cigarette he was going to light when the telephone rang. After a few moments there is a knock at the door. He goes swiftly to open it and* MAUD *comes into the room. She stands looking at him for a moment with a slight smile.*)

MAUD

Hallo, Buffalo Bill. How was your lonely bivouac?

VERNER

(*grinning with pleasure*)

Hi!

MAUD

I'm sure you say that to every taxi you see.

VERNER

Come right in, Princess. Come right on in and put your feet up.

MAUD

(*sitting on the sofa*)

I think it would be more discreet to leave them down.

VERNER

This is great! Just great! I nearly flipped when I heard your voice on the phone just now. I didn't think I was going to see you again for quite a while.

MAUD

No. Neither did I. It seemed a pity.

VERNER

I'd just been talking about you, only a few minutes ago . . .

MAUD

Talking about me? Who to?

VERNER

Felix, the waiter. He's just crazy about you.

MAUD

Is he indeed?

VERNER

He said that you were a lady much enchanted.

254

MAUD

Italians have a flair for romantic exaggeration. Aren't you going to offer me a drink?

VERNER

You bet. What'll it be?

MAUD

Brandy I think, only very little. I have a long drive ahead of me.

VERNER

(*going to the drink table*)

You really are going to drive all through the night?

MAUD

Yes. I'm looking forward to it. There's a moon and there's not much snow left on the pass, the road will be fairly clear.

VERNER

Do you want anything with the brandy? Soda or water or ice?

MAUD

No nothing, thanks just neat. (*A slight pause.*) Why were you talking about me to Felix?

VERNER

I don't know. You said you'd known him in Rome.

MAUD

(*taking the glass he hands her*)

I see.

VERNER

And I guess you were on my mind.

MAUD

You were on my mind too. I talked about you to my son at dinner.

VERNER

What did you say?

MAUD

I can't remember. Nothing very much. Just that I liked you.

VERNER

And what did *he* say?

MAUD

He asked me how long it was before babies started to talk. I replied that in some cases it took a lifetime. (*She laughs*)

VERNER

Why are you laughing?

MAUD

It's been quite a funny evening one way and another. He's in a state of blissful euphoria. The fact of becoming a father has completely transformed him. He had his beard shaved off this afternoon and his hair cut. He even put on a coat and tie for dinner. He had a bottle of champagne and he babbled away like a brook.

VERNER

Are you very close, you and your son?

MAUD

Not really. But we seemed to be tonight. I don't much care for his wife and I think he knows it. She's actually not a bad little thing *au fond* but she's a bit neurotic. I expect having the baby will steady her.

VERNER

What's his name? Your son I mean?

MAUD

Faber. His father's name was Fabrizio and Faber was the nearest I could get to it in English.

VERNER

This Fabrizio—what was he like?

MAUD

Handsome, vain, charming, and badly mother-ridden. She was an old devil and hated me like the plague. I rather see her point now. Being a mother-in-law isn't all jam.

VERNER

Were you in love with him?

MAUD

Oh yes. But it didn't last long. We'd only been married for a year when he was killed in a car crash. That was in 1940. I managed to get myself onto a ship going to Lisbon, and from there back to England. Faber was born in Cornwall.

VERNER

Did you ever see any of them again?

MAUD

Oh yes. After the war was over I came back to Italy to live. I made the old girl fork out enough money to pay for Faber's education. In the last years of her life we almost became friends.

VERNER

(after a pause)

Why did you come back to see me tonight?

257

MAUD

A sudden impulse. I was on my way to Pully to pick up my suit-case from Faber's flat and I was driving along, just out there by the lake and I thought of you sitting up here all by yourself, so I turned the car round and came back. I thought you might be lonely.

VERNER

That was mighty kind of you, Princess. (*He looks at her intently*) I was.

MAUD

Aren't you going to have a drink? To keep me company?

VERNER

Yes, in a minute, after I've asked *you* a sixty-four thousand dollar question.

MAUD

Shoot, pal.

VERNER

Why did you kiss me like you did when you went away before dinner?

MAUD

Another sudden impulse. I'm a very impulsive character. It's often got me into trouble.

VERNER

And you came back because you thought I might be lonesome?

MAUD

Yes. That was one of the reasons.

258

VERNER

There were others?

MAUD

Yes.

VERNER

What were they?

MAUD

They're difficult to put into words. You have to be a master psychologist to dissect an emotional impulse successfully. Just as you have to be an expert watchmaker to be able to take a watch to pieces and put it together again. I'm not an expert in either of those fields. I'm afraid of being clumsy and making a botch of it.

VERNER

I don't reckon you could ever be clumsy.

MAUD
(*with a slight smile*)
Thank you, Verner. Let's hope your reckoning is accurate.

VERNER

You said "emotional impulse." Was that right?

MAUD

Yes. Up to a point.

VERNER

Do you class "pity" as an emotion?

MAUD

Yes. But it was more than pity that made me turn the car round.

VERNER

That's what I was aiming to find out.

MAUD

Well now that you've found out, you can get yourself a drink and let me out of the witness box.

VERNER

(*going to the drink table*)
Okay, lady. You're the boss.
(VERNER *pours some bourbon into a glass, adds ice to it and comes back to her.*)

MAUD

That remark is sadly significant.

VERNER

How come?

MAUD

I've never been to America.

VERNER

It's a great country.

MAUD

(*thoughtfully*)
I suppose American men must like being bossed by their women, otherwise they wouldn't put up with it.

VERNER

(*a little defensive*)
You can't judge Americans by the ones you meet in Europe.

MAUD

I've heard that said before. I'm not quite sure that I believe it. After all the English and French and Italians seem to retain their basic characteristics wherever they are. I can't see why it should be only the Americans who are geographically unstable.

VERNER

You know, Princess. You sure do say the damnedest things.

MAUD
(*repentant*)
I know I do. That's what I meant just now by being clumsy. Please forgive me.

VERNER

There ain't nothing to forgive.

MAUD

I really came back to be a comfort, not an irritant.

VERNER
(*looking at her intently*)
The fact that you came back at all is good enough for me.

MAUD
(*meeting his eye*)
Is it, Verner? Is it really?

VERNER

You know damn well it is.
(*He puts down his drink, takes her drink carefully out of her hand and places it on a table, then he lifts her gently to her feet, puts his arms round her and presses his mouth onto hers. They stand quite still for a few moments, locked in their embrace, then she draws away.*)

261

MAUD

I knew perfectly well that that was going to happen, and yet somehow it was a surprise.

VERNER

(*a little huskily*)

I guess I knew too. But I wasn't quite sure, and I reckon I was a bit scared.

MAUD

Scared?

VERNER

Scared that you'd give me the brush-off, or laugh at me.

MAUD

Why should I laugh at you?

VERNER

I don't mean that I really thought you would. You're too kind to do that, but—well—I'm not the sort of guy who likes to kid himself.

MAUD

(*gently*)

No. I don't think you are.

VERNER

I mean I've seen too many fellars of my age suddenly go berserk and get themselves into trouble, bad trouble.

MAUD

Would you describe that kiss you gave me just now, as going berserk?

VERNER

(ruefully)

Now you *are* laughing at me.

MAUD

These fellows of your own age you talk about. How old are they?

VERNER

(grinning)

Old enough to know better.

MAUD

And this trouble; their sudden madness get them into, this bad trouble—what does it consist of?

VERNER

Oh all kinds of things, making fools of themselves, getting in wrong with everyone, waking up one fine morning and realising that they've been played for a sucker.

MAUD

Do you consider, off hand, that I'm playing you for a sucker?

VERNER

(hurriedly)

No, Princess, you know damn well I don't—I didn't mean that at all.

MAUD

How old are you anyhow?

VERNER

Fifty-five, pushing fifty-six.

263

MAUD

Well I'm forty-four and a grandmother. I'm ashamed of you, Buffalo Bill, running around making passes at grandmothers.

VERNER
(*worried*)

What are we going to do?

MAUD

What are we going to do about what?

VERNER

About this! About us?

MAUD
(*putting her arms round his neck*)

We could always go berserk again.

VERNER
(*after another long embrace*)

You're sensational. D'you know that? You're just sensational.

MAUD

I believe you really mean it.

VERNER

Mean it! I'm crazy about you! (*He moves towards her*)

MAUD
(*backing away*)

No really, Verner, dear Verner, this has gone far enough. We're both behaving very foolishly . . .

VERNER

What's so foolish about it?

264

MAUD

It's my own fault I know. I should never have let it get to this point.

VERNER

Why?

MAUD

Because nothing can come of it, there's no sense in us allowing ourselves to get emotionally involved with each other. There's too much in the way. You know that as well as I do.

VERNER

I don't know any such thing. All I know is I've fallen in love with you, and all I *want* to know is whether you've fallen in love with me. It's as simple as that. Once that's clear all the other complications can be taken care of. Have you?—or rather could you—do you think—be in love with me?

MAUD
(*looking at him*)

Yes, Verner. I think I could, and I think I am. Falling in love sounds so comprehensive and all embracing and violent. It's the stuff of youth really, not of middle-age, and yet—and yet . . .

VERNER
(*urgently*)

And yet—what?

MAUD
(*genuinely moved*)

I don't know. I'm feeling suddenly conscience-stricken.

VERNER

About Anna-Mary?

MAUD

No, not about Anna-Mary. You said yourself earlier this evening
that she was tough and could take it. You're dead right, she's
tough as old boots. If any woman in the whole world asked for
this situation to happen to her she did. I have no conscience whatsoever about Anna-Mary, but you . . . It's you I'm worrying about.

VERNER

Why?

MAUD

I wouldn't like you to get hurt. As a matter of fact I'm not any
too anxious to get hurt myself.

VERNER

There's no fun in gambling on certainties.

MAUD

What exactly do you want of me? Have you thought?

VERNER

No. I haven't had time to think. I only know I want you.

MAUD

You don't know me really at all. You don't know anything about
me.

VERNER

So what? Come to that you don't know so much about me.

MAUD

I think I know enough.

VERNER

That goes for me too.

MAUD

It's not quite so simple as that. We've lived in completely separate worlds, you and I. The standards and codes of behaviour and moral values on this side of the Atlantic aren't the same as those you've been brought up to believe in. I'm not saying that they're either better or worse, but they are profoundly different.

VERNER

It seems to me that people are much the same all the world over, once you get below the surface.

MAUD

That, darling Buffalo Bill, is a platitude and an inaccurate one at that. People are *not* the same all the world over. When you get below the surface of an American you can still find a quality of innocence. There is no innocence left in Europe.

VERNER

What are you trying to say?

MAUD

I'm trying to warn you really. I could never have lived the sort of life I've lived in your country. It wouldn't have been possible.

VERNER

How do you mean the sort of life you've lived? You're scaring the Hell out of me.

MAUD
(*with a slight laugh*)
Oh it hasn't been as bad as all that, but I am, I suppose, what the old-fashioned novelists would describe as "A Woman with a Past."

VERNER
(*drily*)
I hate to have to admit it, Princess, but we have had just one or two of those in the United States.

MAUD

Oh I know—I know. But it still isn't quite the same thing. (*She pauses*)

VERNER

Okay—Okay—let's let it go at that.

MAUD

Nor do I wish to give you the impression that my life has been one long promiscuous orgy.

VERNER

Bully for you, Princess.

MAUD

(*determined to be honest*)
But I have had lovers—here and there along the line.

VERNER

If you'd been in America they'd have been husbands and you could have soaked them for alimony and been a damn sight better off.

MAUD

Oh, Verner! You really are very sweet. (*She kisses him*)

VERNER

C'mon. (*Holding her*) What's all this about?

MAUD

I just don't want you to be disillusioned.

VERNER

That'll be the day.

268

MAUD

I don't want you to wake up one morning like those other fellows, those other romantic innocents, and find that you've been played for a sucker.

VERNER

(*shaking her gently*)

Once and for all will you lay off that kind of talk!

MAUD

Okay, pal. I was only trying to be honest.

VERNER

(*letting her go*)

And get it into your head that it ain't your past I'm interested in, but your future. And that includes me. Do I make myself clear?

MAUD

(*looking down*)

Yes, Verner. Quite clear.

VERNER

Well, that being settled, where do we go from here?

MAUD

(*suddenly laughing*)

What about Rome? It's as good a jumping-off place as anywhere!

VERNER

Whatever you say, Princess.

MAUD

When will you come? This week? Next month? When?

VERNER

This week, next month my foot! I'm coming with you tonight.

MAUD

Verner!

VERNER

In that God damned Volkswagen.

MAUD

It's very small and your legs are so long. I'm afraid you'll be miserably uncomfortable.

VERNER

The seats slide back, don't they?

MAUD

Yes. I'm sure they do . . . (*She breaks off and looks at him*) Oh Verner, do you really mean this?

VERNER

You bet I mean it. What time do we start?

MAUD

(*suddenly turning away*)

I can't let you do this, Verner, I really can't. It's—it's too sudden. You must give yourself more time to think . . .

VERNER

Are you chickening out on the deal?

MAUD

No. It isn't that, really it isn't. I'm thinking of you, not of myself. I meant what I said just now. You haven't any idea what I'm really like. All you know for certain is that I married a Sicilian, had a son in Cornwall and a grandson in Lausanne.

VERNER

I know what Felix said.

MAUD

(*almost crossly*)

Did you consult the nearest floor-waiter before you took on Anna-Mary?

VERNER

(*drily*)

Maybe it would have been better if I had.

MAUD

(*bursting out laughing*)

Oh darling Buffalo Bill, this is ridiculous, it really is. Everything's got out of hand.

VERNER

Now see here, Princess. It was you who went on about the horse and the dolphin and the golden fish. How can I get the golden fish if I'm scared of taking the ride?

MAUD

But you must have loved Anna-Mary once, in the very beginning I mean?

VERNER

I guess I kidded myself that I did, but not for long. She got me on the rebound anyway.

MAUD

The rebound?

VERNER

I was married before, to a girl I was crazy about. (*He pauses*) Then, just after Pearl Harbor, when I'd been drafted into the Navy, she got stuck on another guy and went off with him to Mexico. The divorce was fixed up while I was in the Pacific. When

271

I got home to Minneapolis in 1946 my old man died and I took over the business. Anna-Mary was there, waiting to greet the conquering hero, I'd known her since she was a kid.

MAUD

Was she pretty?

VERNER

Yeah. That's just about what she was, pretty. Her mother and my mother had been in school together. Everybody put their shoulders to the wheel, it was a natural. We got married and lived happily ever after for all of seven months. There was a good deal of dough around even in those days. Then she got pregnant and had herself an abortion without telling me. I'd wanted a kid more than anything so it was a kind of disappointment. She pretended at the time that it was a miscarriage, but I found out the truth later.

MAUD

What did she do that for?

VERNER

I don't know. She was scared I guess. Also she didn't want to spoil her figure. She was always mighty concerned about her figure. I reckon Anna-Mary's eaten enough lettuce in her life to keep a million rabbits happy for a hundred years.

MAUD

Oh, Verner! What a dismal waste of time.

VERNER

You can say that again.

MAUD

And it never occurred to you to break away?

VERNER

Oh yes. It occurred to me once or twice, but it never seemed worth the trouble. We've led our own lives—Anna-Mary and me. She's had her social junketings and I've had my work, and a couple of little flutters on the side every now and again.

MAUD

Well, I'm glad to hear that anyhow.

VERNER

We might have jogged along all right indefinitely if we hadn't started taking these trips to Europe. Europe plays all Hell with women like Anna-Mary, it gives 'em the wrong kind of ambitions.

MAUD

I belong to Europe, Verner. I'm a European from the top of my head to the soles of my feet. That's why I said just now that you ought to give yourself time to think—before you burn your boats.

VERNER

My boats wouldn't burn, honey, they're right down on the waterline anyways. What time do we leave?

MAUD

(*glancing at her watch*)

It's now twenty to twelve. I've got to pick up my suitcase at Faber's flat.

VERNER

I'll pack a few things and meet you in the lobby downstairs at twelve-thirty. The rest of my stuff can be sent on.

MAUD

You're sure? You're absolutely dead sure?

VERNER

Just as sure as I've ever been of anything in my whole life.

MAUD

(*going to him*)

Oh, Verner!

(*He takes her in his arms again.*)

VERNER

As soon as I can get a divorce fixed up, we'll be married and . . .

MAUD

(*breaking away*)

Oh no—don't say that!

VERNER

How come?

MAUD

I don't want there to be any set plans or arrangements or con-
tracts . . . This isn't a business deal. Come and live with me and
be my love for just so long as it works, for just so long as it makes
us both happy.

VERNER

But honey . . .

MAUD

Please, darling Buffalo Bill. We don't want to shackle ourselves
with promises before we start. Don't let any sense of moral responsibility rub the gilt off our gingerbread. You do realize, don't
you, what a shindy there's going to be? Anna-Mary will scream
blue murder. It will be all over Europe and America that Verner
Conklin, the millionaire, has left his wife flat and run off with a

274

dubious Italian Princess who runs a shop in Rome and hasn't a penny to her name.

VERNER

I didn't know you ran a shop?

MAUD

Didn't you? It's quite a success really. We sell curious, rather out of the way things, furniture and what-nots and peculiar jewellery. It's called La Boutique Fantasque. That's one of the reasons I have to be back tomorrow. (*She looks at her watch again*) I must go, darling—I must fly like the wind, if I'm to be back by twelve-thirty. Don't forget your passport. Oh! (*She looks suddenly stricken*) What about Anna-Mary? What are you going to say to her?

VERNER

Nothing much. Just "good night, sweetheart." It's what I've been saying to her for nineteen years.

MAUD

You're not going to explain? You're not going to tell her anything?

VERNER

What would be the sense of explaining? She'll find out in good time.

MAUD

(*conscience-stricken again*)

Will she mind? Really mind I mean?

VERNER

You bet your sweet ass she'll mind. She'll be so hopping mad she'll eat up the furniture.

275

MAUD

Oh, Verner!

VERNER

Don't you worry about Anna-Mary. It's about time she had a real problem to yak about. Get going Baby and be back in that little old Volkswagen at twelve-thirty sharp.

MAUD

Okay, pal! Oh a thousand times Okay! (*She kisses him and goes swiftly out of the room*)

(VERNER, *left alone, walks up and down the room for a moment or two with a springy step. Then he goes to the mirror and examines his face critically. He slaps his hand sharply under his chin in reproval of extra fleshiness. Then, with a sigh, he goes to the desk and sits down by the telephone.*)

VERNER

(*lifting the receiver*)

Hallo . . . Operator . . . Give me the bar please. (*He waits for a moment or two, biting his lip thoughtfully*) Hallo, is that the bar? This is Mr. Conklin in 354 . . . Yeah, I know she's there but I don't want you to disturb her . . . No, there's no need to say I phoned . . . Is the party still going on? . . . Uh-uh . . . The Prince left over an hour ago? . . . I see . . . It's breaking up right now? . . . Thanks . . . thanks a lot.

(VERNER *hangs up the receiver and sits thinking for a minute. Then he quickly takes off his coat and tie, kicks off his shoes, rumples his hair, takes his book from the table where he left it, and stretches out on the sofa. He cocks his ear and listens for a moment then, apparently hearing footsteps in the corridor, he puts his head back, lets the book fall from his hand, and starts snoring gently.*

ANNA-MARY *comes in. She is resplendent in a gown of sapphire-blue satin. She is also wearing a sapphire necklace,*

276

earrings and a thick bracelet to match. She is carrying a hand-bag and a pair of long white gloves. Her expression is grim. She stops short on seeing VERNER *asleep, and it becomes grimmer.)*

ANNA-MARY

(sharply, stamping her foot)

Verner!

VERNER

(waking elaborately)

Why, sweetheart—are you back already?

ANNA-MARY

(disagreeably)

What do you mean, already? It's five to twelve.

VERNER

(sitting up)

Well who'd have thought it? I guess I must have dropped off.

ANNA-MARY

Dropped off! You were snoring like a bull moose.

VERNER

I must have been on my back then. I always snore when I sleep on my back.

ANNA-MARY

(with sarcasm)

That's very interesting, Verner, very interesting indeed. But you'd better go and snore in your own room now, I'm tired.

VERNER

Can I fix you a drink?

ANNA-MARY

(*sinking down into a chair*)

Yes. A bourbon on the rocks. (*She kicks off her shoes and wriggles her toes*) These shoes have been murder all the evening. They get me right across the instep.

VERNER

(*at drink table*)

How was the party?

ANNA-MARY

I just wouldn't know, Verner. I'm so darned mad I can't see straight.

VERNER

What's wrong?

ANNA-MARY

Mariette! That's what's wrong. I'll never speak to her again as long as I live. She's nothing more nor less than a snake-in-the-grass.

VERNER

(*handing her her drink*)

What did she do?

ANNA-MARY

(*taking it*)

Do? She just monopolized the Prince all evening long. I put him on my right naturally and her on the other side of him and she never gave me the chance to say two words to him.

VERNER

Who did you have on your other side?

ANNA-MARY

That stuffed shirt Sir Gerard Nutfield. He's got one of those British accents that I just can't stand. He kept asking me where I *came* from. (*She gives him her glass*) Put some more water in that, it's too strong.

VERNER

(*taking it to the drink table*)

Okay, sweetheart.

ANNA-MARY

My, you look terrible! With no tie on and your hair all mussed up.

VERNER

I'll have it set and waved first thing in the morning.

ANNA-MARY

I suppose that was meant to be funny.

VERNER

(*chuckling*)

Yes, Anna-Mary, that was supposed to be funny. But oh boy! There's better to come!

ANNA-MARY

Have you been drinking?

VERNER

Yeah. Like a fish. A golden fish.

ANNA-MARY

(*coldly*)

And what, may I ask, does that mean?

279

VERNER

It means a Hell of a lot of things. A kid riding on a dolphin for instance.

ANNA-MARY

What?

VERNER
(*pursuing his dream*)
And a flat rock and a little white beach and no tie and my hair mussed up.

ANNA-MARY

You've just gone clean out of your mind.

VERNER
(*cheerfully*)
Way way out. (*He brings her her glass*) Drink up your booze, ma'am, and enjoy yourself.

ANNA-MARY
(*taking it*)
How often have I got to tell you that I just can't stand the word "booze," Verner. It's vulgar and it grates on my nerves. You said it to Maud this evening, and I was mortified.

VERNER

She didn't seem to mind. Maybe her nerves ain't as sensitive as yours.

ANNA-MARY

I should think not, considering the sort of life she leads. You should have heard what Clare Pethrington was telling me about her tonight. I just couldn't believe my ears.

VERNER

That's the one with buck teeth that we had lunch with today, isn't it?

ANNA-MARY

Verner!

VERNER

She looked as if she could eat an apple through a tennis racquet.

ANNA-MARY

I'll have you know that Clare Pethrington is a highly cultured woman. She comes from one of the finest families in England. Her grandfather was the Earl of Babbercombe and her great-grandfather was a close friend of Queen Victoria's. He used to stay at Balmoral every year, regular as clockwork.

VERNER

Bully for him.

ANNA-MARY

Just because she didn't throw herself at your head and butter you up and make you think how wonderful you were like Maud did, you think it's funny to make snide remarks about her.

VERNER
(with deceptive gentleness)

I wouldn't like to make any snide remarks about any of your friends, Anna-Mary, but I would like to say, kind of off the record, that in my opinion this dame we happen to be talking about, is a snooty, loud-mouthed, bad-mannered bitch.

ANNA-MARY

Verner Conklin. I just *don't want* to talk to you any more. And that's the truth. I just don't want to talk to you *any more!* I come back worn out after an exhausting evening and find you lying here drunk. Then you start making silly jokes and saying mean things about people I respect and admire. I'll tell you here and now I've had just about enough of it. You've changed lately, Verner, and it's no use pretending you haven't, you've changed beyond all recognition.

VERNER

You hit it right on the nose, baby. I sure have.

ANNA-MARY

You'd better go to your room, order some black coffee and take an Alka-Seltzer.

VERNER
(gaily)
Did His Serene Highness enjoy his God damned cigars?

ANNA-MARY
(furiously)
Go away, Verner. Go away and leave me alone.

VERNER

Okay . . . Okay . . . That's just exactly what I'm going to do. Good night, sweetheart.

VERNER *picks up his tie and shoes, flings his coat over his arm, looks at her quizzically for a split second, and goes swiftly out of the room.* ANNA-MARY *sits glaring after him balefully as*

The curtain falls

BOOKS BY NOËL COWARD

FEDERAL AID UNDER LSCA
STATE PLAN — TITLE I